VOLCANO WATCHING

REVISED & UPDATED EDITION

By Robert and Barbara Decker
Drawings by Rick Hazlett

HAWAI'I NATURAL HISTORY ASSOCIATION

Published by the Hawaii Natural History Association
in cooperation with the U.S. National Park Service, U.S. Department of the Interior.

Fifth Edition, revised 1996
Designed by Paul Martin
Printed by Hagadone Printing Co.
Honolulu, Hawaii, U.S.A.

ISBN 0-940295-16-4

CONTENTS

PREFACE

Volcano Watching started as a series of weekly newspaper columns which were printed in the Hawaii Tribune Herald. One of our aims was to provide for local readers and visitors alike a glimpse into the mysterious, and often violent, inner workings of the volcanoes that have shaped these Hawaiian Islands. We also hoped to shed some light on the much less violent, but almost as mysterious, inner workings of a volcano observatory and the techniques that are used to decipher the clues that the volcanoes send us. We have included articles on volcanoes in other parts of the world, even volcanoes on other planets in the solar system.

When our first edition was published in 1980, the violent eruption of Mount St. Helens had just shocked the country into a new awareness of volcanoes and their potential for destruction. In the 16 years since then, more than 150 volcanoes worldwide have erupted, killing some 30,000 people. One of the worst disasters, that of Nevado del Ruiz in Colombia, is described on page 70.

In Hawaii, the long-lasting Puu Oo eruption that began in 1983 has continued through 1995, with no loss of life but with great destruction of property. We tell its updated story on page 54.

Robert Decker is a former Scientist in Charge of the Hawaiian Volcano Observatory. Barbara Decker is a science writer, and Rick Hazlett is Professor of Geology at Pomona College. Together they have also produced a series of road guides to National Parks.

HOW VOLCANOES WORK

Volcanoes are such huge features on the landscape that they can't be studied by just one scientific discipline. Volcanology—the study of volcanoes—uses principles and techniques from chemistry, physics and geology, and a new idea has to satisfy all three disciplines.

Volcanoes have their roots deep in the Earth's layers, possibly as far down as 2900 kilometers, and their effects are found high in the stratosphere. Since most of the system is hidden beneath the Earth's surface, much that is known about volcanoes is by inference.

Volcanologists use sophisticated chemical analysis to look at minor constituents in the erupted lava. Geophysical techniques let them hear murmurs in the ground that the ear can't hear, and feel stirrings of the Earth that the body can't feel.

Each year a few more of the Earth's secrets are unlocked, and a few more pieces are added to the intricate and fascinating puzzle of how volcanoes work.

CONTINENTAL DRIFT FORMS VOLCANOES

Back in 1910 an Austrian meteorologist named Alfred Wegener proposed the idea that North and South America had broken away from Europe and Africa, and had slowly drifted apart. He championed this idea for twenty years with attractive arguments like the jig-saw puzzle fit of the continents bordering the Atlantic Ocean, and the continuation of old mountain ranges such as the Appalachians in Eastern North America with similar ranges in Ireland, Scotland, and Scandinavia. He was so zealous that many scientists considered him a crackpot. When geologists determined that the rocks of the ocean floor were too strong to allow the continents to move slowly through them, his ideas were discredited and the theory of continental drift went underground for thirty years.

Then in the 1960s, oceanographers discovered the remarkable pattern and young age of the rocks making up the ocean floor. Drilling in the ocean basins revealed that new ocean floor is being formed along submarine mountain ranges like the Mid-Atlantic Ridge, and that the oldest parts of the ocean bottom, farthest from the Ridge, are less than 5 percent of the age of old rocks exposed on the continents. These sea-floor plate spread apart a few centimeters every year, and the growing gash is sealed from within by submarine lava flows.

During this same decade, other scientists recording earthquake waves from atomic bomb tests discovered a layer of low strength material, probably partly molten, about 100 kilometers (60 miles) beneath the rigid rocky shell of the Earth's surface. The evidence for this layer was its effect in slightly slowing the earthquake waves that passed through it. Knowing the exact location and origin-time of the man-made earthquake waves provided the precision needed to detect this worldwide layer.

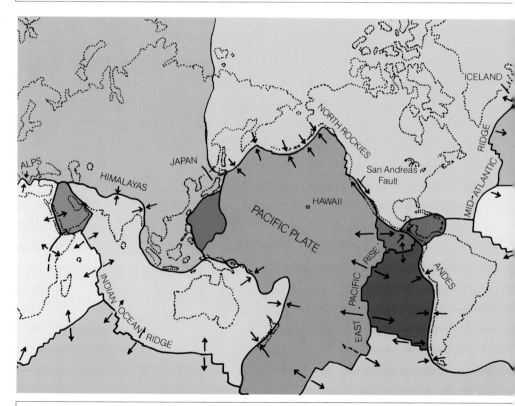

Earth's ever-changing face is broken into numerous crustal plates which, because of powerful internal forces, are in constant motion with respect to one another. Most volcanoes and earthquakes are products of large-scale plate collisions or separations. Solid lines represent major plate boundaries. Arrows show relative motion of the plates at the boundaries. Dotted lines outline continental land masses.

The additional evidence of spreading sea floors, and a slippery layer on which both continental and oceanic plates can slide, quickly led to a general acceptance of the once-discredited continental drift theory. The new twist is that the continents are locked into plates of spreading sea floor and move with, rather than through, the ocean crust.

The test of a new idea is often its usefulness in solving old problems. With regard to the location of earthquakes and volcanoes, the concept of plates of the Earth's crust drifting slowly away from and into one another is a winner. Almost all the action is on the margins of the plates where they pull apart, shove together, or grind past one another.

A few volcanic islands like Iceland mark the highest crests of the spreading oceanic rifts, but most of the ridge is submarine. This huge hidden mountain system which includes the Mid-Atlantic Ridge, Indian Ocean Ridge, and East Pacific Ridge is over 60,000 kilometers long and 2,000 kilometers wide (36,000 miles long, 1,200 miles wide). Drain away the oceans and it would be the greatest mountain range on Earth.

Along the boundaries where plates are coming together, other mountain chains are generated. These form the deep ocean trenches and island arcs of the West and North Pacific including Japan, Kamchatka, the Aleutian Islands, and the mountains along the western edge of North and South America. This belt of great earthquakes and active volcanoes nearly girdles the Pacific and is often called the Ring of Fire.

The hot, weak layer of the Earth upon which the plates drift about appears to be the source of the molten rock that issues from volcanoes. This molten rock ascends along the broken edges of the plates because it is lighter than the cold overlying rocks. Continental drift thus explains both the location and origin of most of the world's volcanoes.

But what about Hawaii? These most well known volcanic islands lie smack in the middle of the Pacific plate. According to continental drift theory they should be as stable and non-volcanic as Kansas. Why are there volcanoes here?

Most of the world's volcanoes are located on the island arcs and mountain chains that border the Pacific, along the grinding edges of slowly moving plates of the Earth's rocky crust. These creaking and leaking edges spawn volcanoes and great earthquakes, and explain the origin of both in relation to continental drift. But what about Hawaiian volcanoes and the Hawaiian Ridge; how can these be explained by motions of the Earth's drifting plates?

One recent answer to this question suggests that new volcanoes keep forming at the present location of the Big Island and slowly move away to the northwest. This is not an entirely new idea, and it has some interesting roots in Hawaiian myths.

Legends tell of the wanderings of Pele, goddess of fire, chased from her former homes on Kauai, Oahu, and Maui by her sister Namaka, goddess of the sea. Pele's present home is in Halemaumau, the crater of Kilauea Volcano on the Big Island. This migration of Pele fits remarkably well with the ages of the islands as determined by geologists. The lavas of Kauai are four to five million years old while those of the Big Island are all less than one million years old.

This similarity of myth and modern science is probably not coincidence. The ancient Hawaiians were excellent observers of their natural world. They must have noticed that the rocks of all the islands are generally of the same type, and they saw them formed during eruptions of Mauna Loa and Kilauea. Add this observation to a knowledge of the concept of erosion and it would be a logical step to infer the relative age of the islands. Those to the northwest are the most eroded; those to the southeast the least.

Perhaps you think the idea of erosion was a bit abstract for the ancient Hawaiians? Consider then this Polynesian saying from Samoa, "Stones rot. Only the chants remain."

HOT SPOTS

Careful geological study reveals that Hawaii's main islands have changed greatly during the last six million years. Frame A shows a map of how the islands may have looked three to five million years ago. Frame B, one to three million years ago. Frame C, the present day Hawaii.

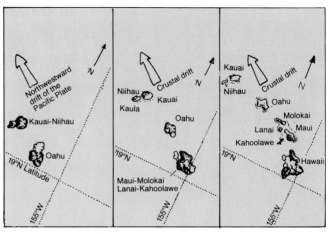

Geologists who first visited the Hawaiian Islands in the 19th century also saw the increasing erosion and age of the islands to the northwest along the Hawaiian Ridge. Although he never visited Hawaii, Charles Darwin recognized that coral-capped atolls were probably the tops of completely eroded and submerged volcanic islands. Midway Island, 2,500 kilometers (1,500 miles) northwest on the Hawaiian Ridge is an example.

The map shows the geologic ages of various islands along the Hawaiian Ridge. The pattern is fascinating, showing a steady aging to the northwest of about five million years for each 500 kilometers (300 miles) in distance from the Big Island.

In 1963 Tuzo Wilson, a Canadian geophysicist, proposed a startling new theory to account for this age pattern of the Hawaiian Islands.

Briefly, his idea is that the Big Island sits over a hot spot in the Earth's mantle that generates molten rock in large batches. This hot, molten rock is lighter than the overlying cold rocks in the rigid crustal plate, and it pushes and melts its way to the surface to form a giant volcano. Meanwhile, according to continental drift, the Pacific Plate is moving slowly northwest over the hot spot at about 10 centimeters (four inches) per year. When the conduits from the hot spot to the volcano get bent over too far, a new conduit forms over the hot spot and a new volcano is born. The previous volcano goes drifting off majestically to the northwest, adding another link to the Hawaiian volcanic chain.

In this theory, Kauai, Oahu, and Maui, in fact all the Hawaiian Ridge, formed over the location where the Big Island is now. A startling idea, but it appears to fit the facts. Looking back to the legend of Pele's wanderings, the hot spot theory implies that she has never left home; instead she has abandoned her used and tattered islands to the sea.

FORECASTING VOLCANIC ERUPTIONS

The only time the weatherman says there is a 100 percent chance of rain is when it's already pouring outside. Similarly, the only time we can say there is a 100 percent chance of a volcanic eruption is after it has begun. Over the past twenty years eruptions of Kilauea Volcano have lasted from less than a day to more than thirteen years, and millions of visitors have been lucky enough to see an eruption in progress.

But what are your chances of seeing an eruption of Mauna Loa if you visit Hawaii for only one week and there is no eruption underway when you arrive? The statistics for the last 150 years indicate a very poor chance; the odds are against you by more than 200 to 1.

Can you improve your chances by knowing what the scientists at the Volcano Observatory know? Definitely. Can you improve your chances to 100 percent? No. That's where the state-of-the-art in volcano forecasting now stands. It can do better than make random guesses about forthcoming eruptions, but it is far from exact.

Weather forecasting has the same problem in trying to predict the weather. Only forecasts based on probability have any validity, but these can be very useful. For example, major storm alerts have saved thousands of lives over the past few years. There can be real gaffes in weather forecasting, though, and anyone in the

prediction business can tell you that it's the wrong calls, not the right ones, that are remembered. The only way to evaluate a forecasting system objectively is to check its performance against random guesses. On this basis, weather forecasting a few days in advance does pretty well, while long range forecasting, months or years in advance, doesn't do much better than average.

Back to volcano forecasting. If someone tells you that there is a 2 percent chance of an eruption starting on Mauna Loa during the next month, that's no big deal—that's the statistical average from Mauna Loa's 39 eruptions since 1832. On the other hand if the forecast is 1 percent or 10 percent, then it's probably based on some of these insiders' tips:

Tilt. During the months or years before an eruption, volcanoes like Kilauea and Mauna Loa slowly swell from an inner accumulation of molten rock, and this causes the ground surface around the summits to tilt outward. This change in slope is not perceptible to the eye, but it can be measured with sensitive instruments called tilt meters. The swelling also causes the rims of the craters to stretch apart slightly and this change can be detected with special surveying instruments.

If the level of swelling is above average or is increasing rapidly, the chance for an eruption is increased above the 2 percent probability. On the other hand if there is little swelling and no tilt changes taking place, the chance for an eruption drops below the 2 percent average.

Earthquakes. As molten rock accumulates within a volcano it exerts pressures which can crack solid rock, causing earthquakes. Swarms of hundreds or even thousands of small, mostly unfelt quakes are recorded on seismographs of the Hawaiian Volcano Observatory during the months or weeks before an eruption. The number, size, and location of the earthquakes are all important in interpreting their meaning with regard to a potential eruption. In general though, the more earthquake activity, the more likely an eruption.

Tremor. A peculiar type of ground vibration detected by the seismographs is called harmonic tremor. This unfelt but continuous shaking of the ground produces a broad, wiggling record on the seismograph that may last for a few minutes to many days. Tremor is always recorded during an eruption, and its intensity varies with the rate at which lava is being poured out. Tremor indicates that molten rock is on

the move, and its occurrence when an eruption is not in progress suggests that molten lava is moving rapidly in underground conduits. A few minutes of tremor is not unusual, but tremor lasting more than 10 minutes is a good sign that an eruption may begin within a few hours.

At the Volcano Observatory, an automatic device registers harmonic tremor and its duration. If the tremor continues for more than 10 minutes, an alarm is sounded in the Observatory and in the homes of the scientists. This fire bell brings the staff running to check the instruments and to prepare for another visit from Pele.

"You can't see any farther underground than I can," snorted the Senator from Nebraska at John Wesley Powell, Director of the newly formed United States Geological Survey. Powell was seeking funds to study the Earth's structure, and the Senator was not impressed.

After 100 years the Senator's comment still has a hard nut of truth to it, but a geologist, in his mind's eye, does see into the Earth. Like doctors who diagnose their patients' problems with stethoscopes and blood pressure gauges, geologists probe the Earth with seismographs and tilt meters. The insight to interpret the vital signs recorded by the instruments, both medical and geological, comes from a growing knowledge about people and our planet.

Scientists at the Hawaiian Volcano Observatory use many techniques to keep track of the inner workings of Kilauea and Mauna Loa volcanoes. Each one gives a few clues about what Pele is up to, and over the years they have revealed some of her habits.

Let's start with the tilt meter, one of the basic instruments used to study volcanoes. Its principle is the same as that of a carpenter's level: tilt up one end of the level, and the bubble of air in the glass tube runs toward the uplifted end. Now increase the sensitivity of the level until you can measure the uplift of a stiff board one kilometer long (five-eighths of a mile) whose end is raised only one millimeter (one-twenty-fifth of an inch). That's a tilt of only one part per million, and that's the sensitivity needed to measure the minute changes in the slope of the ground surface on active volcanoes. It can be done with water-filled tubes several meters in length which have micrometers to measure the change in water level at each end, or with electronic sensors which can detect microscopic motions of a small level bubble.

Once these tilt meters are installed near the summit of an active volcano, the restlessness of the Earth is revealed. Even tides produced in the solid Earth, though smaller than those in the

TILT!

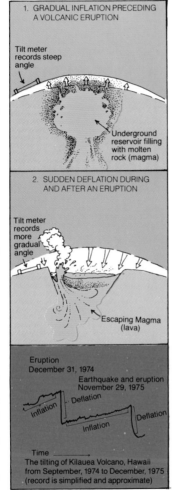

1. GRADUAL INFLATION PRECEDING A VOLCANIC ERUPTION

Tilt meter records steep angle

Underground reservoir filling with molten rock (magma)

2. SUDDEN DEFLATION DURING AND AFTER AN ERUPTION

Tilt meter records more gradual angle

Escaping Magma (lava)

Eruption December 31, 1974

Earthquake and eruption November 29, 1975

Inflation — Deflation — Inflation — Deflation

Time

The tilting of Kilauea Volcano, Hawaii from September, 1974 to December, 1975 (record is simplified and approximate)

sea, can be measured by the small daily changes they produce in the level of the Earth's surface. Tilt meters in stable areas of the world show only these repeating tidal cycles. On active volcanoes, however, much more is seen.

Here is a graph of the tilting of the ground surface at the U.S. Geological Survey's Hawaiian Volcano Observatory between September 1974, and December 1975.

Readings are taken daily on tilt meters at the Observatory on the west rim of Kilauea crater. If the tilt is westward, away from the crater, the volcano is swelling with molten rock like a giant blister. If the tilt is eastward, toward the crater, the volcano is subsiding. The maximum uplift of the center of the blister can be estimated from the amount of tilt.

The tilt pattern for 1975 is fairly simple; slow inflation from January to November 1975, as shown by tilting of the Observatory to the west, then sudden deflation during the eruption in September as shown by tilting to the east. This is the basic pattern of deformation at Kilauea; slow uplift during periods of no eruption as molten rock rises from depths of 50 to 70 kilometers (30 to 40 miles) and is stored in an underground reservoir about three to five kilometers (two to three miles) beneath the summit; then rapid subsidence as an eruption taps the molten rock from the shallow reservoir more rapidly than it is replaced from the deeper source. Notice how the slow uplift resumes after the eruption is over, starting the cycle of change all over again.

The tilt data serve as a kind of blood pressure gauge on the volcano; high levels and rapid increases in outward tilting indicate higher pressures in the molten rock reservoir beneath the summit. Just as high blood pressure is a danger signal in humans, a high level of inflation of the volcano indicates an increasing chance of eruption.

There is no exact level of tilt that triggers an eruption, but most eruptions occur when the inflation is high or is increasing rapidly. Volcano forecasting is not an exact science, but with the aid of tilt meters and other techniques, most eruptions on Kilauea do not come by surprise.

17

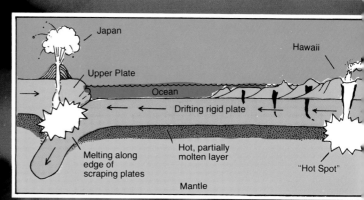

The different origins of Hawaiian and continental-type volcanoes (such as Japan) are shown in this cutaway view of the Earth's interior. Japan's volcanoes result from the friction of several converging crustal plates. Hawaii's volcanoes result from a hot spot beneath a single, drifting crustal plate.

VOLCANOES AND EARTHQUAKES

Volcanoes and earthquakes are underworld partners. Knowledge of this unholy association is not new; in fact the ancient Greeks, whose country has both active volcanoes and destructive earthquakes, believed that "pent up winds" inside the Earth caused both quakes and eruptions.

Scientists today believe that earthquakes occur when rocks being twisted by stresses inside the Earth suddenly break. The energy released by the rupture accumulates for months or years prior to the break, by slow bending of the rocks. A simple analogy is a clock spring; the energy stored in the spring may be suddenly released if the spring breaks from overwinding.

The Earth's major earthquake belts circle the Pacific Ocean and join another belt that extends from Indonesia through the Himalayan Mountains to the mountains bordering the Mediterranean Sea. These same zones have been identified as the places where slowly moving plates of the Earth's rocky shell are grinding into one another.

At the edges of the converging plates the rocks bend and twist before breaking. Weak regions break under low stresses, generating small earthquakes that can only be detected with sensitive instruments called seismographs. Stronger regions break after accumulating greater strain and produce small felt quakes. Huge destructive earthquakes occur when very large fractures suddenly release the bending strain pent up in large volumes of strong rocks. (Substituting the word *strain* for *winds* shows the Greeks were on the right track.) The great fractures are called faults, and can be hundreds of kilometers

long and tens of kilometers wide. The sudden earthquake slip or offset of the fault's sides can amount to a few meters.

But what about volcanoes? About 100 kilometers (60 miles) beneath the rigid rocky plates of the Earth's outer shell is a layer of hot, weak material which is partly molten rock. Where plates converge, one pushes beneath the other and the friction generated by the grinding edges produces enough additional heat to melt even more rock. This molten rock is hotter and lighter than the overlying colder solid rocks and tries to escape upward to the surface. The open fractures produced by the earthquakes make convenient conduits through which the molten rock leaks to the surface. Where it does, rows of volcanoes form into island arcs and mountain chains that make a Ring of Fire around the Pacific.

The Big Island of Hawaii is far from the active rim of the Pacific, yet volcanoes and earthquakes are common here as well. As explained on page 11, these are hot-spot volcanoes; that is, they are formed by a hotter than normal region in the weak layer beneath the Pacific plate. This extra accumulation of molten rock has enough heat and buoyancy to melt and force its way upward through the plate and form volcanoes.

As the molten rock pushes its way toward the surface, the rocks in its path are bent and twisted by stresses until they break, causing earthquakes. A growing volcano forms an enormous weight on the Earth's surface as well as within its own bulk. These load stresses also increase until rocks break. The great Kalapana earthquake in November 1975 resulted from the accumulation of load stresses

added to pressure from molten rock squeezed into the east rift of Kilauea during the eruptions there from 1955 through 1974. This was a period of vigorous activity which included the formation of a new volcanic vent, Mauna Ulu (growing mountain).

In 1975 Mauna Loa Volcano erupted, with lava fountaining from a new fissure across the summit. Rocks on both the northeast and southwest flanks of Mauna Loa were compressed to make room for that new lava-filled fissure. Following the eruption, the summit of Mauna Loa continued to inflate slowly as molten rock accumulated in a shallow reservoir beneath the surface, compressing the flanks more and more. Somewhere, sometime the rocks under that tremendous strain had to snap. They finally did; at 6:13, on the morning of November 16, 1983, a major earthquake jolted Hawaii awake. The rocks beneath the southeast flank of Mauna Loa, about halfway between the summits of Mauna Loa and Kilauea Volcanoes, had suddenly failed.

Foundations were jerked from beneath houses and the people inside were shaken like rag dolls. Large sections of the Crater Rim Road and the trail around Kilauea Crater broke loose and crashed down hundreds of feet to the caldera floor. Eight million dollars in damage occurred in seconds; miraculously no one was seriously hurt.

Which comes first, volcanoes or earthquakes? In Japan you could argue earthquakes; in Hawaii, volcanoes would be a better bet. In truth, both volcanoes and earthquakes are related to the dynamics of the restless earth.

EXPLOSIVE VS. QUIET ERUPTIONS

Why do some volcanoes destroy themselves in violent explosions and collapse, while others slowly and "quietly" build great shields of lava? Volcanologists are still working on the answer to this fundamental question, but a few probable reasons now seem clear.

The amount of gas released in an eruption is one major factor, and the ease or difficulty with which that gas escapes from the erupting molten rock is another important factor.

Gunpowder explodes from the sudden expansion of hot gases released by its combustion. If gun powder is poured into a small open pile and ignited with a flame, it burns without exploding. However, contain that same amount of gunpowder in a tight cylinder of cardboard with a fuse, and you've built yourself a firecracker.

Volcanoes don't burn in the sense of chemical combustion, but the gases dissolved at high temperatures and pressures deep within the Earth are suddenly released when molten rock reaches low, near-surface pressures. If this sudden release of gas is choked back by thick, viscous lavas, an immense explosion can result, hurling rocks and whole mountaintops into the sky.

That is apparently what happened at Mount St. Helens in Washington State on May 18, 1980. Until that morning Mount St. Helens was a steep, conical volcano 9,677 feet high; by nightfall it was an ugly stump of a mountain only 8,364 feet high with a huge new horseshoe-shaped crater about 1-1/2 miles wide, 2 miles long and 1900 feet deep. Most of this decapitation occurred in just the first 10 minutes of the eruption.

Actually not all of the mountain top was really blown into the sky. The great explosion was triggered by a major avalanche of the entire north side of the volcano. This sliding-away of billions of tons of rock suddenly released the pressure on the hot water and shallow molten rock inside the cone, much like opening a pressure cooker lid before cooling the pot. The avalanche unleashed a giant steam explosion that devastated 230 square miles of prime forest. Ten million trees—many of them 10 feet in diameter—were snapped off like toothpicks.

Following the great blast, which was directed northward by the breached north side of the volcano, a huge cloud of volcanic gas and ash rose vertically to 16 miles above the exploding volcano. This ash cloud jetted upward for more than 8 hours as the gas-charged molten rock inside the shattered mountain boiled away. An ashfall 2 to 3 inches thick blanketed central Washington State, and within 3 days the dark ash cloud had reached the east coast.

Let's return to gas content and viscosity, the factors that cause explosive eruptions, and consider each one more closely. Where does the gas in molten rock come from, and how much and what kinds of gases are involved? The gases usually found are steam, carbon dioxide, sulfur gases like sulfur dioxide (choking sulfur smell) or hydrogen sulfide (rotten eggs smell), hydrochloric acid gas (burns your nose and throat), and nitrogen. Steam is generally the most abundant.

The total gas content is only a small fraction of the weight of the molten rock, varying from about 0.25 percent up to about 5 percent. As you can imagine, it's tricky business to try to sample the gases from a violently exploding volcano, so the higher gas contents are at best only approximate. These gas contents given in percentage by weight don't seem very impressive; however, the potential volume expansion of the steam is enormous. If 1 percent water by weight in lava is boiled off at 1,000°C, it forms superheated steam with 170 times the volume of the lava from which it came. Even when reduced to steam at 100°C, it still has 50 times the volume of the lava.

Hawaiian lavas are relatively low in dissolved gases; only about 0.5 percent by weight. Even so, when they suddenly reach a vent from depth the gases boil off in volumes that are 25 to 75 times larger than the fluid lavas. It's no wonder that this enormous volume of suddenly-released gases can spray the fire fountains to heights of hundreds of meters.

If Hawaiian lavas were not so fluid, this rapid release of gas might be choked back until pressures built to explosive levels. Although Hawaiian flows are so fluid that they can run for tens of kilometers down gently-inclined slopes, the tradeoff for more viscous flows would be an increase in the chance of explosive eruptions.

Volcanoes in the island arcs that border the Pacific Ocean—the "Ring of Fire"—generally have lavas with higher gas content and higher viscosity. These factors cause more explosive eruptions, and most of the volcanic debris is fragmental pyroclastics rather than lava flows. This, in turn, builds steep piles of volcanic ashes and cinders strengthened by occasional lava flows, forming the classic concave-upward cones like Mount Fuji in Japan.

Eruptions in Hawaii are often referred to by volcanologists as "quiet" eruptions. This adjective is only valid in relation to the violent explosions of volcanoes on the Pacific rim. Those of you who have heard Pele's rages know the jet-like roar of fire fountains are hardly quiet. The personalities of goddesses are difficult to classify.

Huge explosive eruptions of Mount St.
Helens in 1980 killed 57 people and
devastated 230 square miles of prime
forest.

VOLCANOES: DEAD OR ALIVE?

The activity of volcanoes is almost as diverse as the antics of human beings, and sometimes just as contrary. To describe all these peculiarities, geologists have adopted some human-like terms for the habits of volcanoes: active, extinct, erupting, dormant, and so on. Sometimes these words are used rather loosely; other times their meanings with regard to volcanic action are quite specific. To clarify problems in word-meaning, it's often best to use examples.

What is an active volcano? In the Catalog of Active Volcanoes of the World, published by the International Association of Volcanology and Chemistry of the Earth's Interior, an active volcano is defined as any volcano which has erupted during historic time. That is, any volcano whose eruption of lava or hot fragments has been recorded in written accounts. On this basis, there are about 600 active volcanoes on Earth. Note that active in this definition does not mean that a volcano is presently erupting; only that it has had one or more eruptions in historic time. The number of volcanoes that erupt every year varies from about 40 to 60, including a few like Stromboli in Italy that have erupted almost continuously for centuries.

But historic time; there's the catch. In the Mediterranean, it's over 2,000 years; in Hawaii it's 200 years; and in remote and sparsely settled areas like the Aleutian Islands of Alaska, small volcanic eruptions may still take place without witness or record. There's good reason to suspect that several deep submarine volcanic eruptions take place every year. Even with all the scientific eyes and ears of sophisticated oceanographic instruments today, these deep undersea eruptions occur in splendid secrecy. All this means is that the Catalog of

VOLCANIC ACTIVITY ON HAWAII AND ADJACENT ISLANDS

- ☐ Active volcano with date of latest eruption
- ▨ Potentially active, with date of last probable activity
- ■ Presumed dead volcano

East Molokai

West Maui

Haleakala AD. 1790

Lanai

Kahoolawe

Kohala

Mauna Kea (About 3600 years age)

HILO

Hualalai AD. 1801-02

KAILUA

Mauna Loa (1984)

Kilauea 1996

N

Active Volcanoes is a working list, but it's far from complete and its historic coverage is very uneven from one region to another.

An extinct or dead volcano is one that will never erupt again. Since some volcanoes erupt intermittently over periods of thousands and even millions of years, it's not easy to be sure a volcano is extinct. Some geologists will only classify a volcano as dead or extinct if the period of time since the last eruption is longer than the geologic lifespan of the volcano. By this definition Kohala Volcano is probably extinct, but Mauna Kea is potentially active. Of course, Kilauea, Mauna Loa, and Hualalai are all active volcanoes because they have erupted in historic time.

A dormant volcano is one that is sleeping, so an active volcano can be dormant if it isn't actually in eruption. Sounds like an Abbott and Costello definition, but that's the trap that words can lead to. The period of time between eruptions is called the repose time, another human sounding term. This can vary from days to millions of years depending on the habits and life span of the volcano in question. The average repose time of Mauna Loa over the past 150 years has been four years, while Kilauea's repose time averages 11 to 12 months. In contrast, Mauna Kea's latest repose now exceeds 3,000 years. There's no accounting for sleeping habits!

It often happens that the violence of a volcanic eruption is greater after a long repose. The huge eruptions of Vesuvius in Italy in 79 AD, of Katmai in Alaska in 1912, and Pinatubo in the Philippines in 1991 all occurred at volcanoes that had been dormant for so long that they were not considered active volcanoes. Such potentially active volcanoes, long dormant but not dead, are difficult to identify, but their dangerous nature makes it important to try.

Man sees the world through such a short interval of geologic time that our vision is almost a snapshot of the immense and often terrifying changes that are continually occurring. What seems dead and static in the timespan of a human generation, can be alive with activity in geologic time.

Mauna Loa and Mt. Fuji are two of the world's best known volcanoes. Mauna Loa rises 4,170 meters above Hilo, while Mt. Fuji towers 3,776 meters over Tokyo. Although Mauna Loa is higher, that is not the impression one gets; Fuji appears much the higher and more dramatic of the two.

VOLCANIC LANDSCAPES

This effect is probably caused by the shape of the two volcanoes. Mauna Loa is a dome shaped mountain with gentle convex-upward slopes, while Fuji forms a sharp conical mountain with steep concave-upward slopes. Both are active volcanoes; Mauna Loa last erupted in 1984, and Fuji's last eruption was in 1707. Why are these volcanoes so different in appearance?

The answer lies in the nature of the erupted material, and in the location of the vents. Mauna Loa's erupted lavas have relatively low viscosity, and they run long distances down gentle slopes. This tends to build a volcanic pile that is much wider than it is high. In fact, the ratio of height to width of Mauna Loa is about one to 10; or another way to say this is that the average slopes of Mauna Loa are inclined about 6 degrees. The long rift zones that extend many kilometers northeast and south from the summit caldera of Mauna Loa also tend greatly to widen the volcano. Most of the lava erupted during the last 150 years from Mauna Loa has come from vents on the rift zones rather than the summit. This shapes the mountain into an elongated ridge running along the rift zones, rather than a

symmetrical dome. The name itself—Mauna Loa, long mountain —describes the result.

Geologists call Mauna Loa a shield volcano. The name comes from an Icelandic volcano that is shaped like a warrior's circular shield lying face up on the ground. A German geologist visiting Iceland in the 1800s picked up the name and applied it to all similarly shaped volcanoes throughout the world.

One of the distinguishing features of a shield volcano is the flattening of the slope near the summit so that the whole curvature is convex upward. The origin of this shape is not clearly understood, but it appears to be related to the sagging of the summit region as magma is removed during flank eruptions from the central magma chamber. This process in its extreme form causes the collapse of the summit caldera.

Mt. Fuji's shape is also controlled by the nature of the eruption products and the location of the vents; in both cases these are quite different from those of Mauna Loa. Fuji erupts solid fragments of lava in the form of ashes, cinders, bombs, and blocks; as well as thick viscous lava flows. Most of

these fragments and flows are erupted from the summit crater, but occasionally, as in the 1707 eruption, they are erupted from a vent high on the flank of the main cone. Most of the solid material is hurled into the air during explosive eruptions, and the larger fragments fall near the vent to build a steep-sided cinder cone, much like a giant anthill. The slope of the cinder cone is controlled by the angle of repose; that is, the steepest slope that doesn't slide under its own weight. For angular fragments, this is about 30 to 35 degrees. The thick, slow-moving lava flows, which often alternate with fragmental eruptions, cover and armour the steep cinder-covered slopes, building in time a huge cone of volcanic debris.

Geologists refer to Fuji as a strato-volcano because of the interlayering of volcanic cinders and lavas. Composite volcano is another name for this type, again referring to the mixed nature of the volcanic products. The beautiful concave upward slopes of Mt. Fuji are the classic concept of volcanic form.

Thus a volcano's basic shape is often decided far underground, by the gas content and composition of the magma, and by the geometry of the volcanic conduits which control the location of the surface vents. But only a geologist would be so preoccupied with the importance of the underground foundations when the beauty is in the sky.

Comparative profiles of Mauna Loa and Mt. Fuji volcanoes drawn to the same scale.

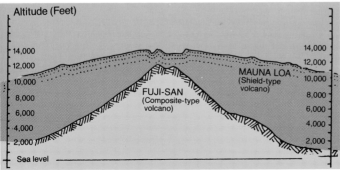

LAVA, ASH AND BOMBS

Volcanoes are dark windows to the interior of the Earth. Since their products are our only direct samples of the Earth's deeper layers, they receive considerable study in Hawaii and elsewhere. Clues left behind in successive layers of volcanic rubble help tell the character and sequence of prehistoric eruptions, and so give us a much broader picture of volcanic events than historic activity can.

Most people think of lava flows as the only product spewed forth from volcanoes. Fortunately for Hawaii that is largely true here; Hawaiian volcanoes, and oceanic ridge volcanoes with their flows deep beneath the sea, do erupt mainly flows of lava.

But on a worldwide basis explosive eruptions are probably more common: volcanic ash and larger solid fragments, called volcanic cinders and blocks, form the major product of observed volcanic eruptions. Lumping together all the sizes of solid fragments, geologists call this volcanic debris *pyroclastics,* which literally means fire fragments. These pyroclastics are made up of magma that is cooled and broken into fragments by expanding gases at the moment of eruption; from fragments of the old crater walls which are ripped loose in explosive eruptions; and from clots of liquid lava thrown into the air which cool during their flight.

Pyroclastic rocks are described by the general size of the fragments. When we speak of volcanic dust, we mean particles as fine as flour. Volcanic ash is more gritty, up to the size of rice; cinders range up to pieces like golf balls; blocks cover everything on up to chunks the size of houses. Volcanic bomb is a special term for block-sized clots of liquid lava thrown from erupting vents. The brilliant arcs on time exposures of volcanic eruptions are the traces of volcanic bombs in flight.

Explosive volcanic eruptions often hurl fragments to great heights, and as the debris falls back to Earth it forms distinct layers blanketing the slopes of the land. The coarser fragments fall first and nearby, while the dust is winnowed away to fall last, sometimes at great distances. These are known as airfall deposits, and can be recognized by their layering and sorting.

The most dangerous and terrifying kind of volcanic hazard is the nuée ardente, or glowing avalanche. This happens when an explosive eruption produces a cloud of volcanic debris so charged with fragments that it is too heavy to rise. This glowing cloud can pour down a mountain at speeds up to 100 km per hour, flattening and burning everything in its path, and even sweeping up and over small hills.

Glowing avalanche deposits pile up on low-lying areas after they lose their speed. The deposits are different from airfall debris, with only vague layering and almost no sorting of fine and coarse fragments. Road cuts in airfall deposits show sharp banding of coarse and fine layers, often of different colors, while cuts in pyroclastic flows show massive deposits that look like pink or buff concrete.

This contrast in explosive debris around a volcano tells something of the nature of its previous eruptions, and gives some clues to the possible nature of future eruptions. For example, at Pompeii, the Roman city buried in volcanic ash from Vesuvius, the beginning of the 79 AD eruption produced several distinct layers of airfall deposits, but the upper layers of ash are more vague and have the character of pyroclastic flows. This would explain the relatively small number of bodies found buried at Pompeii; most people escaped during the early rain of ashes, but stragglers were smothered and buried by the later glowing avalanches.

Hawaiian volcanoes are generally not explosive; they sometimes produce spectacular sprays of lava from the vents called fire fountains, but even these fall back to form slowly moving lava flows. Hawaii was formed—and is forming—from an accumulation of hundreds of thousands of lava flows, each covering only a small fraction of the island.

VOLCANOES AND CLIMATE

Can volcanic eruptions affect the world's climate? Apparently so. Although this question is just beginning to receive serious attention from both volcanologists and meteorologists, preliminary investigations do indicate that there is some connection between major explosive volcanic eruptions and periods of colder weather.

Benjamin Franklin was the first to put this idea into print. Europe had a severely cold winter during 1783-1784 following a major volcanic eruption in Iceland, and Franklin speculated that the eruption may have somehow reduced the sunlight reaching the Earth's surface, thus bringing on colder weather.

There is no doubt that the 1783 eruption in Iceland was of giant size. A great crack, 25 km long, poured forth an enormous volume of basalt. Twelve cubic kilometers of lava spread across 500 square kilometers of land, filling two deep river valleys in the process. For comparison, Hawaii's Kapoho flow of 1960 was only one one-hundredth as much volume and covered only eight square kilometers. In fact, the Laki flow in Iceland, as the 1783 eruption has come to be known, is the largest single flood of lava erupted in historic time.

Although not truly an explosive eruption, the Laki flow was associated with huge emissions of volcanic gases. Sulfurous fumes blanketed Iceland and nearly all the sheep died of fluorine poisoning from eating grass contaminated by the gases. The eruption occurred in a remote part of Iceland. Though no one was killed directly, more than 10 percent of the population starved to death from the loss of livestock

The gases from this great eruption even reached Europe; old accounts speak of dry fogs that were present during the summer and fall of 1783. No wonder that the following cold winter was blamed on nature's volcanic outburst.

Cold winters also followed the major explosive eruptions of Tambora and Krakatau volcanoes in Indonesia in 1815 and 1883. In both cases worldwide temperatures were

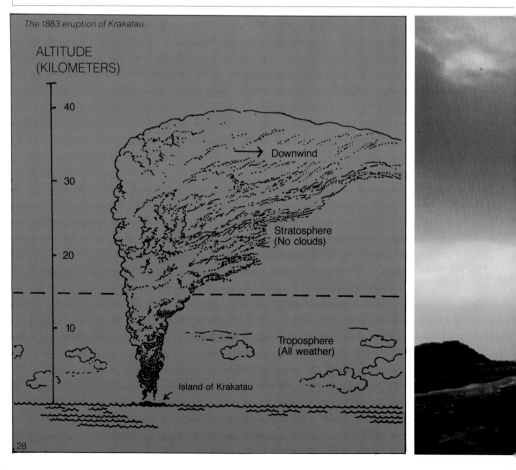

The 1883 eruption of Krakatau.

ALTITUDE
(KILOMETERS)

40

30

Downwind

Stratosphere
(No clouds)

20

10

Troposphere
(All weather)

Island of Krakatau

lowered by a degree or two centigrade for the following one to two years. In 1963 an explosive eruption of Agung volcano on Bali was followed by a year of worldwide stratospheric haze and colder temperatures. Although the Agung eruption was smaller than Tambora and Krakatau, the worldwide weather data in 1963 to 1965 was much more reliable than the older weather records.

The giant explosive eruption of Pinatubo Volcano in the Philippines in 1991 produced a stratospheric haze cloud that reached its maximum worldwide spread by late 1992. Average world temperatures dropped about 0.4 degrees centigrade during 1992-1993.

On the other side of the argument, huge explosive eruptions of Katmai in Alaska in 1912, Bezymianny in Kamchatka in 1956, and Mount St. Helens in 1980, apparently had little noticeable effect on world climate.

Current research indicates several events must occur before a volcanic eruption has much climatic effect. First, the eruption must be a large one, especially one that involves large volumes of sulfur gases. Second, the ash and gases must reach into the stratosphere which starts about 10 km above the Earth's surface. This seems to be necessary because ash and gases at lower levels are flushed out of the air by rainfall. Third, the injection into the stratosphere must be at a location and time of year so that high level winds spread the volcanic debris around the Earth. Equatorial locations appear to be those best suited to affect the whole globe.

It is not yet clear whether the sulfur gases, which form a microscopic mist of sulfuric acid droplets, or the finely powdered volcanic ashes are the more important part of the stratospheric haze layer. High altitude sampling by aircraft during and after a major explosive volcanic eruption will help to resolve this problem.

The exact way in which the stratospheric haze either reflects or absorbs sunlight is under current study, but either way it apparently reduces the sun's warmth reaching the Earth's surface.

Some oceanographers have noted that the amount of volcanic ash in seafloor core samples shows a significant increase before the start of the last ice ages. In this case, nature seems to have her own defenses; fighting fire with ice.

Volcanoes are interesting but difficult features to study. They have their roots deep inside the Earth, and they fling their ash and gases high in the sky. They require study by geologists, chemists, physicists, meteorologists, and oceanographers—all working together. That's part of the fun of it.

ORIGIN OF THE SEA AND AIR

Most astronomers and geologists think that during the early formation of our sun and planets, any original gases and water at the surface of the Earth were boiled away into space by the nuclear ignition of the sun. This hypothesis is based on the scarcity of neon gas in the Earth's atmosphere; a gas which should have been much more plentiful in any original atmosphere.

If the present water and gases in the Earth's ocean and atmosphere were distilled from the interior of the Earth by volcanic processes, the scarcity of neon gas is more easily explained. Neon is an inert element which forms no compounds, and thus is very rare in rocks.

How about the gases that boil out of volcanoes; do they fit the composition of our oceans and atmosphere? Since volcanic gases escape during eruptions it is not easy to determine their composition. Huge volumes of gases propel explosive eruptions, but it is almost impossible to get close enough to sample them.

Indirect methods have proved more successful. Gases in deep submarine eruptions are trapped by the enormous pressure at the bottom of the sea, and are frozen into the glassy rinds of pillow lavas. Samples of these lavas dredged from the sea floor can be carefully analyzed in a chemical laboratory to determine the kinds and amounts of trapped gases.

A few times gases have been collected directly from erupting lava. Scientists at the Hawaiian Volcano Observatory managed this tricky experiment in 1919 when the lava lake in Halemaumau was active. Their results generally support the gas analyses from the deep-sea lavas, and give geologists some confidence about the nature of volcanic gases.

By numbers of atoms, hydrogen is the most important constituent of volcanic gas, followed by oxygen, carbon, sulfur, chlorine and nitrogen. As these elements cool and combine at the surface of the Earth they become water (H_2O), carbon dioxide (CO_2), sulfur dioxide (SO_2), hydrochloric acid (HCl), and nitrogen (N_2). The ratios of these volcanic gases are in remarkable accord with the ratios of water, carbon, chlorine, and nitrogen in the oceans, air, and surface rocks of the Earth. The ratio of sulfur, however, is apparently too high.

Although most of the ratios appear correct for a volcanic source of the Earth's air and water, what about the total amounts? Geologists estimate that about 13 cubic kilometers of new volcanic products are erupted each year on the average. Most of this new lava is never seen, but is required to heal the submarine rifts along the edges of separating plates; for example, along the Mid-Atlantic Ridge and the East Pacific Ridge. Although the gas content of these new volcanic rocks is only about 0.5 percent, that still works out to six trillion tons of volcanic gases each year.

If the Earth has been distilling its air and water from the interior rocks at this rate for its entire 4.5 billion year lifespan, that would account for about 25 percent of the air and water at the Earth's surface.

Puzzling over these calculations, most geologists conclude that volcanoes have been the source of our sea and air, and that very early in the Earth's history, volcanism was much more intense than it is now.

All this leaves two important things unexplained. Where did the free oxygen in the atmosphere come from, and where did all the extra sulfur go? The origin of life on Earth helps to explain both. Plants convert carbon dioxide to free oxygen, generating our life-sustaining air; and small bacteria scavenge the sea and air of sulfur, combining it with iron in the form of insoluble pyrite (FeS_2), better known as foolsgold. If it were not for plants and bacteria our atmosphere would probably be more like that on the planet Venus, a suffocating soup of carbon dioxide and sulfuric acid.

Thanks to volcanoes, early life forms, and time, we have sweet air to breathe, and shining seas to sail.

Present forms of life could not survive conditions similar to those that existed on the young Earth.

HOW HOT IS LAVA?

Watching an erupting volcano is such an overwhelming experience that one's first reaction is usually silent amazement. Questions come later; among the first things most people want to know is how hot the lava really is. There is no simple answer, but we'll try to cover some of the problem.

First a primer on temperature scales. G.D. Fahrenheit, a German physicist, helped invent the modern liquid-filled-tube thermometer about 1700. He put it under his tongue and marked that level as 100 degrees; then into a mixture of ice and salt and marked that zero degrees. Modern physicists jokingly refer to his temperature scale as the one invented by a man with a fever on a very cold day. Nevertheless, Fahrenheit's scale is still commonly used in most English-speaking countries.

A more sensible scale, invented by Anders Celsius, a Swedish astronomer, is based on the boiling and freezing points of water—100 degrees and zero degrees respectively. This scale, called Celsius or centigrade, is the basic temperature scale in the metric system. As we go metric, so we go centigrade, and a balmy day in Hilo is not 80 degrees F, but 27 degrees C.

The hottest lavas erupting from Kilauea have temperatures close to 1,200 degrees C (almost 2,200 degrees F). That's 12 times hotter than boiling water, more than three times hotter than molten lead, but still below the melting temperature of iron (1,535 degrees C).

The temperatures of erupting fire fountains are estimated by using an optical pyrometer, an instrument that compares the color emitted from the glowing lava to the color of a built-in electric bulb. By matching the colors and reading the temperature of the electric filament, the operator can stand at a safe distance and get a close estimate of the erupting lava's temperature. This technique can be used in a rough way by any observer even without a fancy instrument. Temperature and glow-color change together, and color estimate gives a

Using a thermocouple, geologists have been able to measure the temperature of most steaming and fuming areas on Kilauea and Mauna Loa volcanoes. Most steam vents are less than 100 degrees centigrade, the boiling point of water.

temperature estimate: white hot 1,200, yellow 1,100, orange 900, bright red 700, dullest red 500—all numbers in degrees centigrade.

If the lava gets ponded in a lava lake, much more precise temperatures can be measured. By drilling holes in the lava lake crust down to the melt, ceramic rods with thermocouples on the ends can be pushed into the still molten rock. A thermocouple is a pair of wires of different metals twisted together that generate a small electric voltage when heated to high temperatures. By measuring the electric voltage, the temperature can be determined quite accurately.

Making temperature measurements in the cooling lava lakes, and observing the minerals that are forming at these temperatures, has allowed scientists at the Hawaiian Volcano Observatory to learn the complex way in which molten lava "freezes." It doesn't happen at a single temperature the way ice freezes from water at zero degrees C; instead, various

minerals freeze out over a temperature range of about 200 degrees—from 1,200 down to 1,000 degrees C. Crystals of olivine—the green grains on the green sand beaches near South Point, Hawaii—are the first to form, starting at 1,205 degrees C. Feldspar, the small gray crystals seen in some lavas, begin to solidify at 1,180 degrees C. At 1,070 degrees C the lava is about half crystals and half melt, and it becomes nearly solid crystals at about 1,000 degrees C.

The crust on a lava lake is therefore quite different from ice on a normal lake. The ice-to-water contact is a sharp boundary with a temperature at exactly zero degrees C; the lava crust to molten lava boundary is a zone a few meters thick varying from 1,000 up to 1,200 degrees C.

When molten rock is erupted at 1,200 degrees C it has a considerable amount of superheat; that is, the heat above 1,070 degrees C. Some of this extra heat can soften and melt solid rocks with which the hot lava comes in contact. The melting and dripping of the roofs of lava tunnels to form lava stalagtites is one example of this superheating effect.

Actually the fact that hot lava can melt solid rocks in contact with it puts a limit on how hot molten rock can get. If the temperature tries to go above 1,200 degrees, more rock becomes melted and uses up the extra heat. As long as hot molten lava and solid rock are in close contact near the Earth's surface, the temperature is going to be somewhere in the range of 1,000 to 1,200 degrees C.

Such high temperatures are very attractive energy resources. The technology of getting power from molten rock is not yet in sight, but the dream is tempting.

It's not easy to melt a rock; you would be hard put to find a way to do it in your home workshop, even with a plentiful supply of electricity or propane gas. Lava is fairly close to common glass in composition, so your best bet would be to set up a glassblower's furnace for your rock melting project. How then does nature produce so much molten rock? What is the heat source, and where is the furnace?

There may be more than one source of heat. A list of possibilities includes: 1) The original heat of formation of the Earth 4.5 billion years ago. 2) Heat from disintegration of natural radioactive elements. 3) Tidal friction in the Earth's interior. 4) Some other process of which we are unaware. Frictional heating from the moving plates could also be listed, but this merely begs the question of what drives the plates; it must in itself be some form of internal heat engine. The total energy is neither created nor destroyed; it's simply transferred into different kinds of energy—heat into motion, motion into heat.

But back to the list. Could the Earth have been hot enough when it formed so long ago that the lava's heat is part of that primordial temperature? Without additional heat sources, the answer to that is no. In fact, Lord Kelvin in the last century calculated that the Earth could be no older than about 25 million years to still have enough original heat to supply the Earth's present volcanism and other heat losses from the interior. The catch is that Lord Kelvin didn't know about radioactivity.

Heat from the breakdown of natural radioactive elements appears to be a prime candidate for volcanic heat. However, don't run from the nearest chunk of basalt; its radioactivity is trivial, less than many other common rocks. How then could it melt from its own radioactive heating? The answer has two parts—geologic time and great insulation.

The heat producing elements in basalt are uranium, thorium, and potassium 40. Each of these elements forms only about one millionth part of an average basalt lava. All together, their radioactive heat production is only one millionth of a calorie per gram per year. Yet with perfect insulation, that is enough heat to melt the basalt in three hundred million years.

The crustal plates of the Earth are about 100 km thick, and rock is a good insulator. Imagine your home insulated with a blanket of rock wool some 60 miles thick! Not a perfect insulator, but almost.

Most geologists today think that the Earth's internal temperature is maintained largely by radioactive heating. Volcanoes work as a kind of safety valve; as heat builds up, rocks at depths of about 100 km slowly begin to melt. Since this molten rock is lighter than the surrounding rocks, it rises or forces its way to the surface, venting heat in volcanic eruptions. If too much heat is lost through volcanic action, the molten rock is used up and volcanism stops, at least until enough geologic time passes to renew the process. The times involved are millions of years, not the few years or hundreds of years between individual volcanic eruptions. These shorter pulses are but an eyeblink compared to the long-term heating and cooling of the Earth's inner layers.

Daily tidal forces of the sun and moon slowly bending rocks up and down cause friction heating. Some geologists believe this to be an important source of internal Earth heat. Since we have only poor knowledge of how much tidal energy is used up by ocean currents compared to that spent in bending rocks, this potential source of heat energy is still largely speculative.

Although today we know of one or more heat sources that can sustain volcanoes on the Earth for 4.5 billion years, it is wise to remember Lord Kelvin's mistake. He was not aware of radioactivity. What may we be ignorant of?

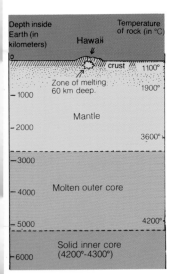

A cross-section of the Earth, from the crust to the center of the core. Estimated temperatures of the interior are indicated on the right.

GEOTHERMAL POWER

This is one of those things that's tough to explain. You could toss it off with a simple statement like "Geothermal energy is the heat inside the Earth," or you could write a textbook about it that would put everyone to sleep. Something in between seems needed, so let's tackle it.

First, it's important to understand the subtle difference between energy and power. Heat is one form of energy, and there's an immense amount of it inside the Earth. In deep mines and drillholes throughout the world, it's a general observation that the deeper you go, the hotter it gets. For each kilometer of depth the temperature increases about 20° to 60° centigrade, depending on the region. The heat energy contained in just the upper 10 km of the 50 United States is estimated to be eight million billion billion calories. That's eight with 24 zeroes after it; if it were accessible it would supply our present energy needs for the next 100,000 years. If it were accessible; that's the catch.

Power is the rate at which energy is used. It's measured in watts. One kilowatt, about the amount of power used by an electric toaster, is 0.24 kilogram calorie per second. The calories in the food you eat in a day would power that toaster for about three hours. Power then is the key word. We have a power crisis in the world, not an energy crisis. There is plenty of diffuse energy around; the trick is to turn it into power.

The heat flow escaping from inside the Earth is a small fraction of a watt through each square meter of the Earth's surface. To light a 100 watt bulb you would have to collect all the heat energy escaping through a square area with 40 meter sides, and convert that to electricity with 100 percent efficiency—an impossible task. Therefore, for geothermal power

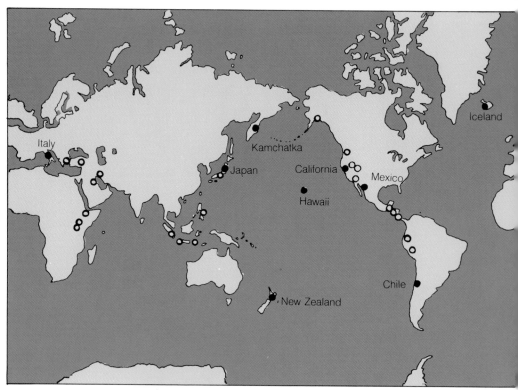

Geothermal power is a major source of energy in several countries. Dots show some important geothermal centers currently in operation. Circles indicate localities where geothermal power is a potential future energy source. In a world where fossil fuels are rapidly being used up, geothermal power is becoming an increasingly valuable natural resource.

to work, some special situation must exist or be created that will allow the Earth's heat energy to be concentrated into a small area.

Natural or man-made reservoirs of steam or hot water within the Earth's crust that can be concentrated into a drillhole provide just this needed special situation.

In non-volcanic areas you would have to drill to depths of six or seven kilometers just to reach boiling temperatures. However, in young volcanic areas where molten rock has brought up heat from deeper levels, it's possible to drill into rocks and steam reservoirs heated to 100° to 350° centigrade. The secret of geothermal power is to locate these shallow reservoirs of steam and hot water, and to tap their pent-up energy with a series of drill holes.

Exploring for geothermal power reservoirs is similar to exploring for oil, except that the geologic setting is volcanic rather than sedimentary. Once geologists and geophysicists think they have found in the subsurface a zone of porous rocks filled with steam or hot water, it must still be drilled to prove it. There are lots of dry holes; it's no business for the fainthearted. Sometimes the wells are hot enough but the formation is tight and steam can't be produced fast enough to turn a turbine. Sometimes the porous reservoirs are small and soon depleted.

But when a good geothermal reservoir is discovered, it's a real bonanza. At The Geysers area in northern California, Pacific Gas and Electric Co. is generating over 1,000 megawatts of electric power. That's enough for San Francisco, and it's the cheapest power around. The field has been going strong for more than 30 years, but steam production in some places has diminished. There must be an end to it somewhere, but it's not yet evident. That's both the good and the bad news about geothermal power; it's such a young industry we can't really evaluate either its potential or its problems.

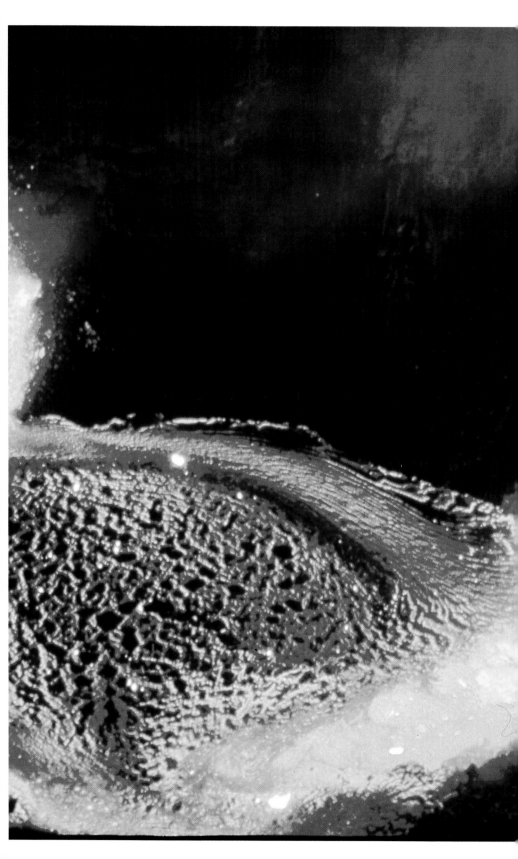

VOLCANOES IN HAWAII

A combination of fortunate circumstances makes Hawaii a nearly ideal place for watching volcanoes. For one thing, Kilauea and Mauna Loa are relatively active, with a moderate-sized eruption every year or two, as opposed to other volcanic areas which may have huge eruptions but on a time scale of hundreds of years.

These volcanoes are also relatively safe. Because of the composition of Hawaiian lavas, eruptions here are of the "effusive" type with spectacular fire fountains and very fluid lava flows. The explosive eruptions common elsewhere are extremely rare in Hawaii, so volcanologists can make their observations close to the erupting volcano and volcano-watchers can experience at close range Nature's grandest show.

Thanks to the foresight of T.A. Jaggar who founded the Hawaiian Volcano Observatory in 1912, Hawaii's volcanoes have a long history of observation. This continuity of research through many eruptive cycles has made possible major contributions to volcanology and to eventual eruption forecasting.

Hawaii National Park was created in 1916, taking in most of Kilauea and a large strip of Mauna Loa including the summit. One of the staff's most important functions is to interpret this unique volcanic scenery to the public, but they are also responsible for protecting the visitors from the capricious volcanoes (and protecting the volcanoes from the over-enthusiastic visitor).

Add to all this Hawaii's felicitous year-round climate, and it's easy to see why Hawaii's volcanoes are the most accessible, best studied, and most enjoyable in the world.

HOW OLD ARE THE HAWAIIAN ISLANDS?

Age is a slippery term. It's best to pin down the definition before committing numbers into print. Do we mean absolute age, relative age, behavioral age, or still some other aspect of birth, life and death?

Absolute age is one that can be measured in years or days or centuries—some specific units of time—and needs no comparison to other things. Relative age, in contrast, needs no specific numbers, but exists in relation to the age of some other being or object. For example you can say that Mary is 45 and John is 50 (absolute ages), but it might be more tactful to say that Mary is younger than John (relative ages). Or if an old timer, volcanic or human, is bursting with activity, his behavioral age belies his absolute age. With these age concepts in mind, how old are the Hawaiian Islands?

The ancient Hawaiians recognized the relative ages of the islands; that volcanic fires had left Kauai and Oahu and had migrated to Hawaii. The legends clearly say that Pele moved from Kauai to Oahu and on to Maui, finally taking up her present home in Halemaumau. The ancient Hawaiians were keen observers; this relative age sequence is still valid today.

J.D. Dana, an American geologist with a U.S. Navy exploring expedition in the 1840s, was the first to write about the apparent increase in the age of the Hawaiian Islands as you sail northwest. From the change in weathering and decomposition of the lavas, and the erosional destruction of the islands by streams and waves, Dana correctly established their relative ages.

No further progress was possible until methods of radioactive dating were discovered, allowing absolute ages to be measured. The principle is simple and elegant, although the actual laboratory measurements require painstaking precision and expensive equipment. Certain atoms are radioactive; they break down at very slow but consistent rates into different atoms that are finally stable. The breakdown is accompanied by emission of radioactive radiations and particles that can be measured, thereby establishing the number of radioactive atoms present. This amount is called the parent element.

By careful chemical analysis, the number of daughter atoms of the breakdown process can also be established. By knowing the ratio of the parent and daughter atoms, and the rate of radioactive

breakdown, the age of a rock or mineral can be established. The concept is similar to a financial savings account. If you know the ratio of your original savings dollars to the number of increased dollars, and also know the interest rate, you can calculate how long your money has been on deposit—the age of your savings account.

One of the most useful radioactive clocks in rocks is a potassium atom that contains a total of 40 sub-atomic particles in its nucleus. Potassium 40 breaks down into argon 40 gas at such a slow rate that it takes over one billion years for half of the original potassium 40 atoms to disintegrate. Most volcanic rocks contain small amounts of potassium 40, and their age since they cooled and hardened can be measured by the number of the argon 40 atoms trapped in the rock during its lifetime. This breakdown of potassium 40 atoms into argon 40 atoms, like so many sand grains spilling from the top of an hourglass to the bottom, gives lavas a built-in timer.

Ian McDougall, an Australian geologist, was the first to measure the absolute ages of Hawaiian rocks in 1964. To geologists his ages seem young; to others they seem ancient. Leaving out the details this is what McDougall discovered:

Ranges of ages in millions of years of the major lavas on various Hawaiian Islands.
Kauai: 3.8 to 5.6
Oahu: 2.2 to 3.4
Molokai: 1.3 to 1.8
Maui: 0.8 to 1.3
Hawaii: less than 0.7

Kauai is nearly six million years old! What rages must Pele have in store, now that her true age has been revealed?

Millions of years
into the past

Hawaii
(Still growing)

Maui forms

Molokai
forms

— 1 —

— 2 —

Oahu forms

— 3 —

— 4 —

Kauai forms

— 5 —

Recorded history begins,
Hawaiians arrive and
Captain Cook reaches Hawaii
(all within the width
of the line)

Great ice ages

Quaternary Period Begins

Origin of man in Africa
(Date uncertain)

Extinction of the dinosaurs,
65 million years ago

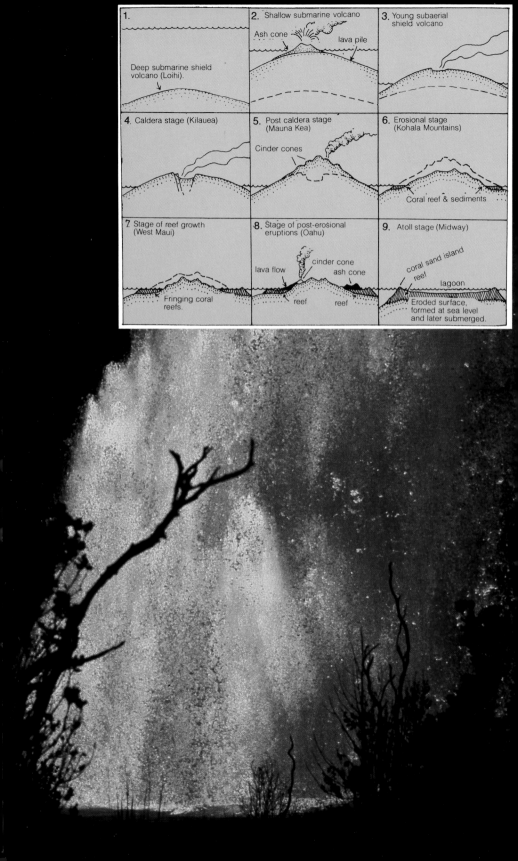

1.

Deep submarine shield volcano (Loihi).

2. Shallow submarine volcano

Ash cone

lava pile

3. Young subaerial shield volcano

4. Caldera stage (Kilauea)

5. Post caldera stage (Mauna Kea)

Cinder cones

6. Erosional stage (Kohala Mountains)

Coral reef & sediments

7. Stage of reef growth (West Maui)

Fringing coral reefs.

8. Stage of post-erosional eruptions (Oahu)

lava flow   cinder cone   ash cone

reef   reef

9. Atoll stage (Midway)

coral sand island

reef

lagoon

Eroded surface, formed at sea level and later submerged.

LIFE STAGES OF HAWAIIAN VOLCANOES

Volcanoes are almost as singular—and as marvelously unpredictable—as human beings; but in spite of highly individual characteristics, they can be said to pass through the general stages of birth, youth, maturity, old age and death. Some even indulge in another human folly, a last fling, when it has been assumed that life has almost flickered out.

Hawaiian volcanoes are born on the deep ocean floor, below four to five km of water. Quiet outpouring of lava goes on intermittently—and largely undetected—for thousands of years, as the mound builds closer to the surface of the ocean.

When the growing volcano is within about 100 m of the surface, the gas in the magma is able to expand and explosive activity begins, producing large steam explosions which spray ash high into the air. Ash falls are easily washed away, but once out of water the eruptions continue as the relatively quiet, effusive eruptions we see today on Kilauea. Lava flows continue to armour the growing mountain until it is safe from wave erosion.

The last time a Hawaiian Island emerged from the sea in this manner was about a million years ago, when the Kohala volcano broke the surface of the ocean with the first rocks of the Big Island. Recent evidence shows a new seamount building silently in the ocean about 25 km south of Hawaii, but it is not expected to reach the surface for thousands' of years.

Toward the end of their youthful growth period the tops of most Hawaiian volcanoes collapse to form large sunken-in craters known as calderas. Volcanism is still very active at this stage, however, and a long period of repeated collapse and refilling of the caldera follows. This is considered to be the mature stage, and can go on for thousands of years. Kilauea and Mauna Loa are both in this mature, caldera stage.

There is still much that is not known about how calderas form, and similarly, no one knows for sure why the caldera phase gradually comes to an end, though it is assumed to be related to the cooling of the magma reservoir as eruptions decrease. Whatever the reason, the caldera finally becomes filled and in the last stage of activity a caldera no longer exists. (This sequence is different for Hawaiian volcanoes than for volcanic chains on the continents; for those, like Mt. Mazama in Oregon with its Crater Lake, the formation of a caldera is usually the last event.)

In the old-age stage a steeper cap is built on top of the shield, covering the filled caldera. The late stage eruptions contain lavas of different chemical composition than the earlier ones, particularly with increased sodium and potassium. This change can take place gradually as it seems to have done on Mauna Kea and Haleakala, with new types of rocks appearing along with the older ones without much interruption of activity. On others, like Kohala, volcanic activity stops for thousands of years and then starts again with wholly new rock types. Most late-stage eruptions are more explosive than the typical Hawaiian shield-building eruptions, and form steep cinder cones. This explains why Mauna Kea has a much steeper summit than Mauna Loa; Mauna Kea is clearly in its old age.

After this stage most volcanoes have reached the end of their activity, and erosion by streams and waves works to wear them down. A few volcanoes, though, come to life for a last explosive fling after very long periods of quiet. Diamond Head and Punchbowl are highly visible examples of late volcanic revivals on Oahu. In the next thousands of years there could be additional eruptions on Oahu or on Maui; nature likes surprises. Erosion wins in the end though. With the long passage of time, rain, streams and waves wear everything down to sea level.

Not all Hawaiian volcanoes go through this whole sequence. They can skip a phase, or die prematurely at any stage. Hualalai, for example, seems to have skipped the caldera stage and is slipping into old age without an adolescence. This is a necessarily simplified account of a complicated subject; for more details, and good reading, see **Volcanoes in the Sea**, by Macdonald, Abbott and Peterson.

PAHOEHOE AND AA

Anyone who has spent a few hours hiking in Hawaii knows from first-hand experience that lava flows are of two distinct types: smooth flows where walking is a pleasure, and blocky, jagged ones where walking is a nightmare of lacerated boots and painful falls.

These flows are so characteristic of Hawaii that they are known all over the world by the Hawaiian names—pahoehoe for the smooth flows, and aa for the jumbled ones. When these words were first introduced into scientific literature by C.E. Dutton in 1884, they met with strong opposition from some writers who objected to the use of such "barbarous" terms, but were quickly adopted anyway.

Pahoehoe has a smooth, billowy surface, often with a wrinkled or ropy appearance where a "skin" has started to form and has been dragged along by the more fluid lava underneath. These are rapidly moving flows, which sometimes divide to surround an obstruction leaving an island— or kipuka—of vegetation in the middle of a flow. The rivers of pahoehoe quickly crust over and leave streams of lava moving in tunnels under the crust. When the supply of lava feeding the stream stops, the lava drains out leaving an empty tunnel or lava tube. These are very common in Hawaii—probably the best example being the Thurston Lava Tube in Hawaii Volcanoes National Park, where hundreds of visitors walk through every day.

An aa flow advances in a different way. Commonly there is a central river of molten rock five to ten meters across, flowing at speeds of 5 to 50 km per hour depending on the slope. The flow then oozes out on all sides from this central stream and forms slowly-

blocks in much the same way that a batch of fudge will start to sugar and quickly become chunky. Hawaiian lavas in general are very fluid, and so travel much faster than lava flows in other parts of the world. Usual rates in Hawaiian eruptions are 10 to 100 meters per hour, while lava flows

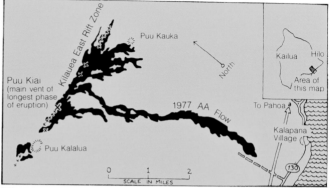

Kilauea's east rift zone erupted from Sept. 13 to Oct. 1, 1977. Initially, most of the flows were fast-moving streams of pahoehoe. Later, almost all of the lava changed to aa. The intriguing pattern made by the flows is shown in black. +'s mark the principal eruptive vents.

advancing dark lobes of cooling lava rubble riding on a molten but unseen core.

The lava blocks tumble down the steep front of the advancing flow, sometimes giving a glimpse of the glowing interior, and are slowly overridden.

The growing edges and fronts of the flow look like giant slow-motion bulldozer treads moving out, down, and under as the mass spreads forward. As a result the surface is a layer of angular jagged fragments, each covered with tiny sharp spines.

Most flows emerge from the vent as pahoehoe and somewhere downslope change to aa. Change in the other direction doesn't happen, though sometimes pahoehoe will flow through a tunnel under an aa flow and emerge looking like a continuation of the aa flow. The chemical composition of both kinds of lava is the same; the change occurs when a pahoehoe flow starts to cool and loses some of its gas content. The number of internal crystals increases and the flow starts to break up into jagged

in most other regions commonly move only a few meters per day.

This fluidity lets Hawaiian lava run freely down mountainsides forming flows which can be very long—some are as long as 50 km—and comparatively thin. Pahoehoe flows here average about one to two meters in thickness and aa flows about three to four meters. The long-lasting eruption of Kilauea at Puu Oo has produced immense volumes of both aa and pahoehoe. In the early phase of the eruption, with intermittent high fountains, the flows were mostly aa, while the later, more continuous eruption produced mainly pahoehoe flows.

Old Hawaiian trails favored the pahoehoe flows, and for good reason. The thin crust quickly disintegrated even under bare feet, leaving a smooth easily visible trail to follow. Where a trail had to cross an aa flow, smooth rocks were carried, sometimes for many miles, and placed as steppingstones to make walking more comfortable and less hazardous. Many of these

steppingstone trails can be seen today, particularly in the Kona district where aa flows from Mauna Loa reached the sea.

History has reversed the preference: today's roadbuilders would much rather work across an aa flow where the clinkers crush to an acceptable road bed, than deal with an exasperating pahoehoe flow where a bulldozer at best kicks up awkward slabs of rock and at worst is in peril of dropping through the surface into a lava tube.

Whether trail or road, Pele will probably cover them both in time.

Tunnels partially filled with molten lava up to seven miles long formed on Kilauea volcano during the Mauna Ulu eruptions.

LAVA TUBES

The establishment of Hawaii National Park in 1916 could not have been accomplished without the foresight and perseverance of two men. One was Thomas Jaggar, founder of the fledgling Hawaiian Volcano Observatory. The other was Lorrin A. Thurston, noted politician and publisher whose influence on the Hawaiian press helped popularize the national park idea in Hawaii.

A keen volcano watcher, Thurston spent much time on the Island of Hawaii. In 1913, he participated in an expedition that led to the discovery of a future tourist attraction, the Thurston Lava Tube. The expedition was prompted by the curiosity of Thurston's young niece, Margaret B. Shipman. The Shipmans owned a home in the Volcano community, and for some time had been curious to learn whether or not a nearby cave led to an outlet near the rim of Kilauea Caldera.

Together with Thurston and Jaggar, Miss Shipman set out to search for the phantom outlet. She recalled that it was a test of endurance for her to keep up with the men because of the cumbersome dress that she wore on the journey through the dense fern forest. Eventually the explorers came to the south side of a small crater, and looking across observed a large, dark opening on the opposite wall. They descended into the crater and made their way along its floor to the north wall to stand under a gaping hole well beyond their reach.

After rigging a ladder the next day, the three climbed into a prehistoric lava tube and found it filled with lava stalactites and stalagmites. Jaggar quickly christened the tunnel "Thurston's Cavern" and subsequently "Thurston's Lava Tube."

Today, hundreds of thousands of visitors walk through Thurston Lava Tube every year. Although the beautiful stalactite and stalagmite formations have been destroyed by vandals and souvenir collectors, a visit to the tube is still an interesting experience.

Since the days of Jaggar and Thurston, much has been learned about the nature of lava tubes. During the Mauna Ulu eruptions in 1970-1971, active lava tubes were studied by two Volcano Observatory scientists, Don Swanson and Don Peterson. Major tubes were developed by the cooling of solid crusts over molten lava streams in pahoehoe flows. Tubes up to 12 kilometers long were formed, with hot lava flowing through them at rates of one to six km per hour. The tubes began as narrow passageways one to three meters deep, but gradually enlarged to at least 13 meters deep. This enlargement was probably due to downward erosion of the channel floor by the molten lava. Because the sides of the tubes acted as excellent insulators, the lava cooled very little as it flowed through them.

This insulating effect allows pahoehoe flows to travel many kilometers. Although the eruption of Kilauea at Puu Oo began in 1983, it was not until 1986 that flows reached the 11 kilometers to the sea. The early phase of the eruption consisted of a series of intermittent high lava fountains. The aa flows from the fall-back of these fountains reached only about 6 kilometers downslope.

In July, 1986 the vent of the east-rift eruption of Kilauea shifted 3 kilometers down rift. The new eruption site was called Kupaianaha, a Hawaiian word that means surprising, and one of the most surprising things about the new vent was that it erupted slowly and continuously, in contrast to the rapid but intermittent eruptions earlier at Puu Oo. Like the tortoise versus the hare, the slow-moving but continuous pahoehoe flows from the new vent formed lava tubes and reached the sea within a few months.

IS HAWAII SINKING?

Changes in sea level are of more than passing interest to islanders, but the slow rates at which they usually proceed make them more curious than alarming.

Before the Kalapana area was covered by lavas from Kupaianaha in the late 1980s, you could walk along a shoreline of prehistoric pahoehoe flows. At several places large tree-mold holes could be seen that were submerged by incoming waves. Those trees did not grow in the sea, so the coast must have subsided or sea level must have risen.

On the Kona Coast there are ancient Hawaiian game boards carved in the smooth pahoehoe lava flows that are now awash at high tide.

These observations and a careful study of the tide gauge records from Hilo, Honolulu, and mainland U.S. ports, have led geologist James Moore to estimate the present rate of submergence of

the Big Island at 4 millimeters per year. That's about one inch every 6 years and more than a foot per century.

Not all the evidence points to sinking. Honolulu is built on an emerged reef about 25 feet above present sea level, and in other places around the Hawaiian Islands there are many examples of emerged and deeply submerged reefs. Since reefs form in warm, shallow water just below sea level their elevation after thousands or millions of years is a good indication of sea level change.

Why do shorelines rise or fall? There are at least two major causes: either the land rises or sinks with respect to the Earth's center, or there is a change in true sea level with respect to the Earth's center. It is not always possible to sort out these two effects from one another. If the land sinks and sea level drops at the same rate, the shoreline remains stable.

Changes in true sea level can occur by addition or removal of large amounts of water from the ocean. This occurred several times during the ice ages. Colder climate piled up great ice caps on the high latitudes of the continents and sea level dropped as much as 200 to 400 feet below its present level. Melting all the ice that still exists on Greenland and Antarctica would raise sea level about 200 feet above its present level. Climates have been fairly stable for the last 10,000 years, and true sea levels have changed only a few feet in all that time. However, present evidence suggests that ice ages can come and go rather rapidly, and cause drastic sea level changes within a thousand years.

Changes in the volume of the ocean basins are apparently affected by continental drift, and slow changes in true sea level of more than 1,000 feet without glacial additions or subtractions are attributed to these ponderous processes.

So much for true sea level changes. What causes the land itself to sink or rise? Beneath the rigid shell of the Earth's drifting plates, there is strong evidence for a zone of hot, plastic rocks. This zone is about 40 miles down beneath Hawaii and is the source region for the lavas which have built the islands. As the volcanoes grow, their enormous weight pushes down on the rigid crust and it slowly sinks into the plastic zone below. This adjustment in balance is just the same as would occur if you climbed onto an iceberg floating in the ocean. It would sink a little to get back into adjustment. But the plastic layer is much less fluid than water, so the sinking takes thousands to millions of years.

The slow horizontal movement of the plates also has its own ups and downs. Generally as a plate moves away from the ocean ridge where it formed it gets cooler and thicker, and thus subsides. The general elevation of the deep sea floor confirms this idea; it is most shallow at the ocean ridges and gets progressively deeper on

Waipio Valley, on the windward side of the Kohala Mountains, was cut by stream erosion when sea level was much lower than it is now. Streams cut V-shaped valleys, and the steep valley sides would meet in a notch about 300 feet below present sea level. As the shoreline was submerged the valley was filled by flat deposits from the drowned stream.

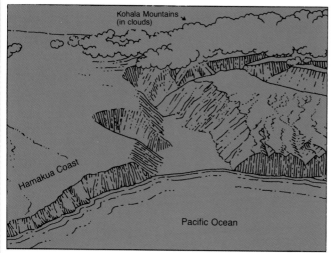

both sides. As Hawaii moves northwestward from the East Pacific Ridge it rides gently down slope into the deeper ocean basin.

Uplift beneath the active volcanoes also occurs from the intrusion of liquid rock which does not escape to the surface. The more shallow the region of intrusion, the more local the uplift. The opposite process is also possible. Removal of liquid rock from beneath the surface, perhaps to feed a major lava flow, will result in subsidence of the land above the region of removal.

With all these possibilities for sinking or rising, the most remarkable fact is the relative stability that exists. Only during major earthquakes that cause a sudden up or down shift in the shoreline do we become aware of the not-so-solid Earth.

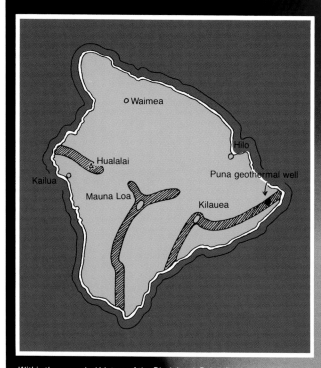

Within the recorded history of the Big Island, Pele's fire has erupted out of several narrow land belts, called rift zones. The summit calderas of Kilauea and Mauna Loa have also been prolifically active. The volcanic areas are shown as shaded strips on the map. Most potential geothermal energy sources on the island lie within these active areas, where suitable groundwater is present.

GEOTHERMAL POWER IN HAWAII

Hawaii is the right location for finding geothermal power. Molten rock from 60 km beneath the Earth's crust rises to the surface and builds the island. These erupted lavas lose their heat rapidly, providing tempting but probably not practical sources of energy. However, beneath the volcanic summits and along the rift zones, molten rock accumulates at shallow depths of two to four km, and is not all erupted to the surface. These shallow bodies of molten rock heat the ground water, creating reservoirs of steam and hot water.

So much for theory. What has drilling proved? In 1973 a deep hole was drilled at the summit of Kilauea for research purposes. The objectives were to understand better the location of the shallow magma chamber, and processes by which heat is transferred from the molten rock to the ground water system. It was not a prospect hole for geothermal power.

Much interesting scientific data was discovered in this drill hole. For example, the well encountered dry rocks at surface temperature to a depth of 450 meters. At 500 meters, still 600 meters above sea level, ground water was encountered and the temperature rapidly rose to about 90°C. Temperature decreased again to about 60°C at 900 meters, and then began increasing rapidly. The maximum temperature was 137°C at the

1,262 meter bottom of the hole. The rise in temperature near the well bottom was very steep, indicating the presence of molten rock another two to three km down. The irregular temperature gradient indicates that water is circulating at depth and transporting heat, but the high water table and occurrence of tightly cemented rocks at depth indicate a low permeability. The well was just reaching the most interesting depths when the drill reached the limits of its ability to penetrate deeper.

The results of this drilling experiment suggest that volcanic summits are not the best targets for geothermal prospecting. This is certainly fortunate for Kilauea, for no matter how badly we need power, the National Parks must remain inviolable to industrial development.

What about the rift zones? Geophysical surveys in 1973 indicated a promising area in the lower east rift zone between Pahoa and Pohoiki. This area was explored by deep drilling in 1976 with encouraging results. Below 500 meters the water in the well is at or near the boiling point curve. Boiling temperature increases with increasing pressure, and reaches about 340°C at the 1,950 meter bottom of the hole. By removing the overlying water column in the well, the pressure at depth is reduced to near-surface pressures, and the hot 340°C water in the bottom of the well flashes to steam and rushes out the open borehole with the roar of a jet engine.

Although the flow rate of the steam indicates that the reservoir is not as permeable as the one at

The Geysers in California, the Hawaii discovery well produced 2 to 3 megawatts of electrical power for several years during the 1980s.

More production wells were drilled in this area in the late 1980s and now supply a commercial 25-megawatt power plant. Since the Island of Hawaii only uses about 100 megawatts of electricity, this is a significant source of electrical power.

Geothermal power development in Hawaii has encountered severe growing pains. Besides the problem of possible degradation of the environment, the questions of the actual size of the resource and of who owns the underground hot water are still unanswered. Even so, people have taken sides and the groups are sharply divided.

It's never easy, and it's not always right, to take a step in a new direction. Geothermal prospecting and development will continue to be a controversial issue in Hawaii for years to come. One can often learn from developments in other countries. Both Iceland and New Zealand have major geothermal power projects: in Iceland over 60 percent of the homes are heated with hot water produced from geothermal wells. Although space heating is no great problem in Hawaii, it truly is in Iceland. It's clear that Iceland would not be the prosperous country that it is without geothermal power.

In New Zealand a major portion of their electric power is generated by geothermal steam. The noise and smell are under control, but not eliminated. Everything has its price.

REGROWTH OF PLANTS AFTER VOLCANIC ERUPTIONS

To walk across a glistening black lava flow a year or so old is always a sobering reminder of the destructive power of nature; but to see in a crack or tree-mold on that lava flow a tiny cluster of bright green ferns is an even stronger reminder of the tenacity of life. Nature seldom provides brand new land on which to study the patterns of establishment of plant life, but occasionally a volcanic eruption does just that.

The 1959 Kilauea Iki eruption which devastated an area of about 1,200 acres provided an ideal opportunity. Over a period of nine years after the eruption a detailed study of the Devastation Area was made by two biologists, Garrett Smathers and Dieter Mueller-Dombois, working under grants from the National Park Service and the National Science Foundation, with investigations made every year.

They were especially interested in finding out the sequences and rates at which plant life forms arrive on new surfaces; how volcanically damaged vegetation recovers; and what environmental factors limit plant invasion and recovery. Another important question they wanted to answer was whether exotic plants have an edge over native plants in establishing colonies on new volcanic surfaces.

They divided the Devastation Area into six different habitats to study: the crater floor, the cinder cone, an area of spatter with tree snags, a pumice area with tree snags, a pumice area with surviving trees, and a thin ash-fall area on the Kau Desert. Every year they photographed, measured and counted plant life in a specific plot within each habitat.

The first two habitats—the crater floor and the cinder cone—had no residue of life, but within the first year the lava cracks of the crater floor showed touches of green. The cinder cone was slower to cool since heat was rising through the loose pile of pumice so no life appeared there until the third year, but then in the same sequence as in the crater. Smathers and Mueller-Dombois found that on these new volcanic surfaces algae always arrived first and lichens second. Ferns and mosses became established either first along with the algae, or in a group with the lichens. Native woody seed plants came next, with exotic plants last.

The cracks in the lava floor were especially favorable environments since they provided some shade, collected additional rainfall, and sometimes additional moisture from vapor steaming from below. Often a colony of algae, ferns and moss would start in a crevice and later seed plants would take root with them. By the ninth year of the study, some cracks were crowded with plants while a nearby crack that looked identical would be empty. This suggests that the presence of the first group of plants improved the moisture relations, making it easier for other plants to take root with the colony than alone.

The pattern of arrival of plant life was different in the other habitats studied, which had some organic residues ranging from dead Ohia snags to scarcely damaged plants, depending on distance from the eruption. There seed plants appeared early, with exotic plants among the first to become established.

The devastated area, resulting from the 1959 eruption at Kilauea's summit, is shown by the dotted area on this map. Greater concentration of dots indicates thicker cover of pumice and cinders. The cover varies in thickness from about 2.5 centimeters near the margin to over 10 meters near the cinder cone (X), where the major fire fountain erupted. The solid black area indicates the lava lake that filled the floor of Kilauea Iki Crater to a depth of 120 meters.

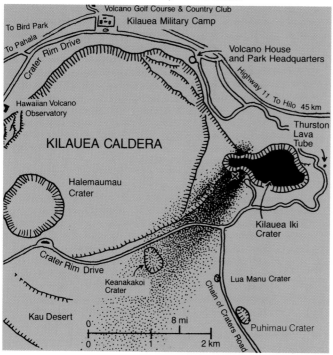

The survival of existing plants depended on several factors. The depth of the pumice deposit was most important, but the temperatures also were critical. Ohia trees survived a pumice deposit up to 2.5 meters thick where it wasn't too hot, but only about 10 cm where the deposit was hot spatter. In general, trees recovered only when their trunks were covered to half their height, while many shrubs and herbs survived under the pumice layer even when broken or buried.

One of their most interesting discoveries was that the native woody plants and ferns were in no way affected by competition from exotics. Even in places where exotics had appeared first; by the ninth year of the study they were being replaced by natives; even the ubiquitous blackberry was no competition for a native woody creeper.

If you're interested in more details about this intriguing study, read "Invasion and Recovery of Vegetation after a Volcanic Eruption in Hawaii" by Garrett A. Smathers and Dieter Mueller-Dombois, National Park Service, Scientific Monograph Series number five.

KILAUEA'S PUU OO ERUPTION

Pele is a mischievous goddess. What better way to start a New Year than to keep the volcano scientists on full alert? So began 1983.

Just after midnight on January 2 the tremor alarm at HVO was triggered, and geologists on call hurried to the observatory. Seismic recorders were dancing with both small earthquakes and tremor, the continuous background vibration that is characteristic of magma moving in underground conduits. The tremor was greatest on seismometers located on Kilauea's east rift, and the tiltmeters were showing rapid deflation of Kilauea's summit area. All signs indicated that magma was being injected into the east rift from Kilauea's summit magma chamber. As Hawaiian legend would explain the process, Pele was on the move again by her "road underground."

The east rift, a zone of weakness within the flank of Kilauea Volcano, has been the location of thousands of eruptions during the lifespan of the volcano—20 in the past 150 years. As the magma chamber beneath the summit of Kilauea inflates, the pressure of the molten rock increases. When this pressure exceeds the strength of the surrounding rocks, the volcano splits apart a few feet and magma wedges into the fracture, forming a nearly vertical blade-like dike. These dikes are generally a few feet wide, several miles long, and extend from depths of 2 or 3 miles to the surface or near-surface.

The process of magma forming a dike is called an intrusion, and shallow intrusions often occur in the rift zones without erupting to the surface. From 1977 to 1983 there were 12 shallow intrusions into Kilauea's east rift zone, and only 2 of these, in 1979 and 1980, broke out into eruptions.

That past behavior pattern suggested that the New Years intrusion was probably just another one of Pele's underground forays, but that was not to be the case. Hours passed, the tremor and earthquakes continued and slowly migrated down the rift, indicating the underground progress of the tip of the growing dike. The summit continued to deflate at a rate of about 1/4 inch per hour, giving some measure of the amount of magma that was pushing into the underground crack.

Geologists in the field moved down the rift to stay in the area above the tip of the extending dike, where a surface breakout was most likely to occur. Finally, past midnight on January 3, and 24 hours after the intrusion began, their wait was over; the crack broke the surface on the rift about 10 miles east of Kilauea Caldera. Steam roared out, followed by jets of molten red lava. The longest and largest rift eruption in Kilauea's recorded history had started.

The early fissure eruption produced spectacular lines of lava fountains called "curtains of fire." These later localized to a single vent which erupted intermittently, producing high lava fountains that were visible for miles. Episodes of lava fountaining as high as 1,500 feet lasted several hours to a few days, and alternated with periods of about a month when there was little or no activity.

By 1986 the vent had built a large cone of lava spatter that reached a height of 836 feet, and was given the name Puu Oo (hill of the Oo bird). Typical fountaining episodes each produced about 15 million cubic yards of lava; part falling back to build the spatter cone, but most flowing away in rivers of lava down the flank of Kilauea. Those flows, mainly aa lava, destroyed several houses and covered many undeveloped house lots.

After the 48th episode of fountaining in 1986, a new vent opened 2 miles downrift from Puu Oo. Gas continued to escape from Puu Oo, while pahoehoe lava poured slowly but steadily from the new vent at a rate of about 1/2 million cubic yards per day, closely matching the resupply rate of magma to the summit chamber beneath Kilauea.

This phase of the eruption lasted until 1992 when new outbreaks near the base of the old Puu Oo cone took place. These vents have built a lava shield about 200 feet high on the uprift side of Puu Oo, where a small but active lava lake has formed deep within the old crater. Pahoehoe flows from this latest phase have roofed over into lava tubes which reach the sea on the west side of the great 1983-1996 (and still growing) lava field.

This long-lasting eruption has added two new words to the language of volcanoes: Vog—volcanic fog—formed from the gas emissions of Puu Oo; and laze—lava haze—formed in the steam cloud where lava pours into the sea. Vog is an aerosol of sulfuric acid, and laze an aerosol of hydrochloric acid. Nasty stuff.

The coastal entrance and visitor center of Hawaii Volcanoes National Park at Wahaula was burned and overrun by lava in 1989, and the village of Kaimu, with its famous black sand beach, was covered in 1990. The eruption has so far destroyed 180 homes and caused property

damage nearing $100,000,000. On a brighter note, the lava entering the sea is forming huge new deposits of black sand, and someday new black sand beaches will be part of the legacy of the Puu Oo eruption.

The Kalapana area has been devastated, but the people forced to move persevere. "No one has been hurt," they say, "and, after all, this is Pele's land."

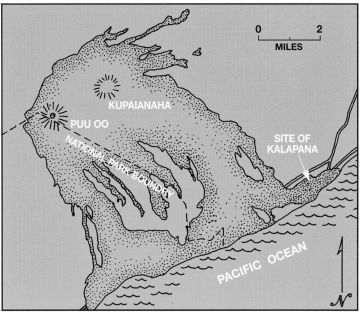

KUPAIANAHA

PUU OO

NATIONAL PARK BOUNDARY

SITE OF KALAPANA

PACIFIC OCEAN

0   2
MILES

N

Lava flows from the 1983-1996 (and continuing) eruption of Kilauea.

HOW ARE THINGS ON MAUNA LOA?

On March 30, 1984 the night sky over Hawaii Volcanoes National Park glowed all around the horizon, with the look of sunrise and sunset happening at once. The cause of this visual drama? Towering Mauna Loa Volcano and the Puu Oo vent of neighboring Kilauea Volcano were for a few hours in simultaneous eruption—only the second time this century that both volcanoes have erupted at the same time.

The star performer this time was Mauna Loa; Kilauea had been erupting almost once a month for more than a year, but Mauna Loa's last eruption had been in 1975 and the one before that in 1950. Besides, Mauna Loa is such an immense mountain—the largest active volcano on Earth—that it was bound to assume center stage.

In general terms this eruption of Mauna Loa was not unexpected. For the last ten years scientists at the Hawaiian Volcano Observatory had been carefully monitoring Mauna Loa's increasing earthquake activity, and measuring the inflation of the mountain as the magma chamber swelled beneath its summit. Both trends seemed to be accelerating in 1983, leading Observatory scientists to publish a forecast of a probable eruption within the next one to two years. Forecasting is a risky business, but fortunately in Hawaii the public is knowledgeable enough about their volcanoes to react with alertness and curiosity instead of with panic.

The eruption forecast came true on March 25, 1984; at 1:30 AM a red glow lit the night sky over Mauna Loa's summit caldera, where the first lava fountains broke to the surface in a "curtain of fire" along a fissure. Accompanying earthquakes and tremor were so strong that the astronomical telescopes on Mauna Kea, 30 miles away, could not be stabilized for observations.

Over the next few hours the vents migrated out of the crater and down the northeast rift zone. As the lower vents opened, the vents higher upslope—including those in the caldera—shut down. The main vents soon established themselves in a zone about a mile long, at the 9,400 foot level of the 13,677-foot mountain.

The lava fountains rose to about 50 feet; not high by Hawaiian standards—fountains on Kilauea sometimes exceed 1,800 feet—but the flows that poured out were voluminous and fast moving.

The main flow headed northeast toward Hilo, covering nine miles the first day. Walls of cooling lava built up into levees on the edges of the flow, and the 1,130°C

Mauna Loa flows nearing Hilo.

molten rock coursed down the channel between them.

Volcano watchers from all over Hawaii—and volcanologists from all over the world—converged on the Big Island to see or to study this spectacular and potentially dangerous eruption.

The flow slowed somewhat as it advanced, but was still confined to a narrow channel. Concern mounted in Hilo—especially at night, when the advancing red-hot flow and the fume clouds above it, glowing orange from the reflected light, looked even closer than they were. As the flow moved through the rainforest above the town, hundreds of acres of native forest were crushed and burned, and explosions of methane gas that accumulated near the edges of the flow could be heard in Hilo.

Civil Defense was ready. There was no panic, but residents quietly began packing their most treasured belongings in case a shift in direction or speed of the flow made a sudden evacuation necessary.

On March 29, when the advancing flow had reached to within five miles of the outskirts of town, Hilo was granted at least a temporary reprieve. About ten miles upstream one of the levees confining the channel collapsed, and lava was diverted into a second parallel flow. A few days later, just as the second flow caught up with the first, another collapse occurred. At the same time the lava production was beginning to slow somewhat, and the lava was becoming more viscous.

In the following days more collapses and diversions took place even farther upslope; the flows were now spreading out instead of advancing relentlessly downhill. By April 14 no active lava flows extended more than a mile from the vents. On April 15 the eruption ended, and the threat to Hilo, from this eruption anyway, was over. Not forever, of course—the whole Big Island is built up of old lava flows like a giant pile of candle drippings—but a time span of hundreds of thousands of years is a little easier to be philosophical about.

The 1984 eruption was by far the most extensively studied in Mauna Loa's long history. Those studies and others since are chronicled in a new scientific book called Mauna Loa Revealed (see page 84), published in 1995. But what about future eruptions? They will surely occur, but at this time (April 1996) the earthquake and inflation data do not suggest any imminent new eruption. The latest forecast suggests a 50% or better chance that the next Mauna Loa eruption will occur before the year 2008. Mauna Loa watchers, don't hold your breath.

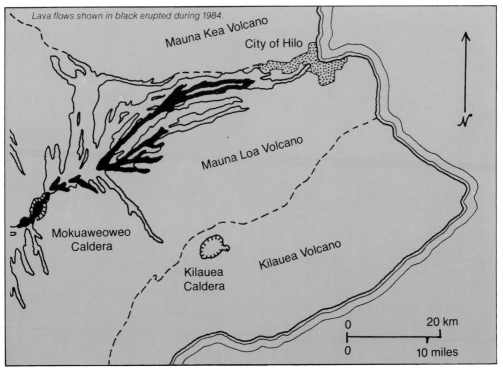

Lava flows shown in black erupted during 1984.

Mauna Kea Volcano

City of Hilo

Mauna Loa Volcano

N

Mokuaweoweo Caldera

Kilauea Caldera

Kilauea Volcano

| 0 | 20 km |
| 0 | 10 miles |

MAUNA KEA'S GLACIER

Schoolchildren in New Hampshire have little difficulty understanding what the Ice Age must have been like. They see a small sample of it every year when the land is locked up in ice and snow for several months; no bare ground can be seen, only the largest rocks protrude above the icy surface, and the Earth is frozen hard for three to six feet down.

But how to explain in Hawaii what the last great Ice Age was like, when the summit of Mauna Kea was covered with a glacier?

There is good evidence that during the last Ice Age about

15,000 years ago, Mauna Kea had a permanent ice cap that covered an area of about 28 square miles. It had a maximum thickness of 350 feet, though the average was probably about 200 feet. Many of the large cinder cones on the summit would have protruded through the ice.

At the same time ice covered all of Northern Europe and much of Northern Asia. On the North American continent, thick ice sheets covered almost all the land above the latitude of New York City. Some of these great continental ice sheets were as

much as 5,000 feet thick. South of the ice margins, the high mountains had many more glaciers than they do today.

A glacier forms when yearly snowfall doesn't have a chance to melt before the next year's storms start. As the annual layers accumulate to greater depths, the snow in the lower layers is transformed from light snowflakes to granular snow like little lumps of ice, and finally is compacted into a dense blue ice. Under the weight of its own thickness and the influence of gravity, the ice slowly begins to flow, moving downhill and outward from the greatest thickness.

In high mountainous areas streams of ice form that flow down valleys and are called, logically enough, valley glaciers. Broad mounds of ice that spread in all directions are known as ice sheets if they are large, and ice

caps if they are relatively small. It was an ice cap that crowned Mauna Kea, with lobes extending down on all sides—several to 11,000 feet. The most extensive lobe was on the south slope, above Pohakuloa, reaching down to 10,500 feet.

There are places on Mauna Kea where the glacier left marks that are still visible today. A glacier carries large amounts of ground-up rock fragments and debris as it moves slowly downhill. When it starts to melt and retreat, it leaves a ridge of this debris where the edge of the glacier had been. These ridges are known as moraines—terminal moraines parallel to the ice front and lateral moraines along the edges of the lobes. The moraines above Pohakuloa can be seen clearly today, even from the Saddle

Road. Especially visible is the V-shaped loop of the moraine left by the glacier, at the head of the gorge cut by the Pohakuloa stream.

The fragments carried by a moving glacier also abrade and polish the rock under the ice. In small areas on Mauna Kea's summit striations are found on rock ledges, and other rocks are polished into the rounded knobs fancifully known as roches moutonnées because of their resemblance to the rounded forms of sheep.

Did Mauna Loa have a glacier also? Possibly, but we can't be sure. In the Ice Ages Mauna Loa was in a youthful growing stage and was probably as much as 2,000 feet lower than it is today; just about at the lower limit of Mauna Kea's ice. At any rate, there have been so many later

eruptions of Mauna Loa that glacial evidence, if any, would long ago have been covered over.

All this is not as far-fetched as it sounds. Glaciers exist today in equatorial regions of South America in the Andes mountains, and of course, the highest mountains in the world, the Himalayas with their huge glaciers, exist in the tropical belt of Asia. Climate, latitude and altitude are all controlling factors. Gordon Macdonald estimated that if Hawaii had an increase in average rainfall of only two inches, or a drop in average temperatures of only a few degrees, a year-round snow cap would form on the high summits. The accumulation of snow from year to year would soon form a glacier, and Mauna Kea's icy past would live again.

This artist's conception shows what the summit of Mauna Kea might have looked like during the last ice age. The Pohakuloa glacial lobe is shown at left-center.

THE KALAPANA EARTHQUAKE OF NOVEMBER 29, 1975

Twelve minutes before five o'clock on the morning of November 29, 1975, a major earthquake struck the southeast coast of Hawaii. A group of campers at Halape, a coconut grove along the shore of Hawaii Volcanoes National Park, were near the center of the violence. The campers had been awakened by a sharp but smaller quake about an hour before the main shock, but most had gone back to sleep.

At 4:48 a.m. the main earthquake unleashed its pent-up fury. Most of the campers at Halape were able to struggle up during the first shaking, but were soon thrown to the ground as the violence increased. Some clung to trees or rocks for support. They were trapped between huge rockfalls tumbling down the cliffs behind the grove, and the rising water from the first of a series of tsunamis that almost immediately followed the earthquake.

The second sea wave swept everyone inland through the grove, as far as 100 meters. Most were washed into an old lava crack about five meters deep and 10 meters wide along with broken trees, the wrecked shelters, horses and rocks. Several smaller waves churned over the crack; one survivor likened the experience to being "inside a washing machine." Two persons and four horses were killed. The thirty other campers miraculously lived through the ordeal.

In Hilo the earthquake shattered windows and cracked walls, but caused no major injuries. Twenty minutes later a series of small tsunamis with a maximum height of 1.7 meters surged in and out of Hilo Bay, sinking four boats and damaging several others.

At 5:30 a.m. an eruption began from a 500-meter-long fissure on the floor of Kilauea Caldera, and continued intermittently during most of the day.

Were the earthquake, the tsunamis, and the eruption connected; and, if so, in what way? Scientists at the Hawaiian Volcano Observatory and the University of Hawaii consider that these events were closely related to one another, and that the cause goes back many years before the sudden release of violence.

Volcanic activity along the east rift of Kilauea Volcano has been relatively intense since the Puna eruption in 1955. Every time a new lava-filled crack formed along the east rift to feed an eruption, the rift zone was wedged apart. This widening of the rift caused its sides to be squeezed into compression much like a wedge driven into a log squeezes the wood alongside the wedge before splitting occurs.

There is good evidence that this process was indeed happening. From 1965 to 1970, a survey line from the top of Holei Pali to the coast, near the steep switchbacks on the Park Highway west of Kalapana, was remeasured many times. During this five-year period the line actually shortened by 35 centimeters, clearly showing that the south flank of the east rift zone was being pushed into compression by the lava-filled cracks wedging into the rift.

In 1974, geologist Donald Swanson, who was conducting the surveys, put the following statement into print: "Some of the data suggest that the Hilina fault system is poised for another episode of subsidence, with only minor additional ground displacement needed to trigger it . . . we anticipate a subsidence event of unknown magnitude in the not-too-distant future."

That event was the magnitude 7.2 earthquake which split a 50-kilometer-long buried fracture beneath most of the southeast coast of Hawaii. The whole coast heaved suddenly outward a meter or more, causing the land to subside and the sea floor to rise. The earthquake waves were produced by the sudden rupture which released the pent-up compression of the south flank of the east rift. The tsunamis were caused by the violent displacement of the sea floor which raised and tilted the sea surface over hundreds of square kilometers just off the southeast coast. The cause of the summit eruption is less clear, but it apparently vented from a major fracture related to the outward movement of the entire southeast flank of Kilauea.

The whole pattern of eruptions along the east rift, and the cycles of inflation and deflation at the summit of Kilauea were changed by the shake-up of this major earthquake. For the next 6 years magma continued to move underground but only twice found its way to the surface in an eruption. Now, though, things seem to be back on the track. Two small eruptions at Kilauea's summit in 1982, and the major Puu Oo eruption on the middle east rift zone (1983-1966, and continuing), show that Pele is no longer in hiding.

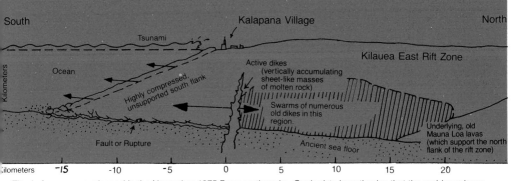

Titanic forces were released in the November 1975 Puna earthquake. Geologists hypothesize that the sudden release of forces climaxed a long period of slowly accumulating strain in Kilauea's east rift zone. A simplified, hypothetical model of the earthquake is shown in this cutaway section of the rift zone.

A Hawaiian Volcano Observatory scientist operates a geodimeter, a laser beam device used to measure distances.

TODAY AT THE VOLCANO OBSERVATORY

Scientists at the Hawaiian Volcano Observatory like to quote the remark made by Dr. Thomas Jaggar, founder of the Observatory, who said: "The two hardest things about running a Volcano Observatory are keeping the staff from getting bored between eruptions, and from getting hysterical during eruptions."

Looking back at the long history of scientific observations here, it can safely be said that with all the frantic activity during Kilauea's frequent—and Mauna Loa's less frequent—eruptions, the hysteria level has been just about zero. Boredom has proved to be just as inconsequential; the biggest problem is finding time to get everything done.

The Observatory's main scientific function is to study the five volcanoes (Kohala, Mauna Kea, Hualalai, Mauna Loa, and Kilauea) that form the Big Island. In doing so, HVO makes a basic contribution to volcanology in general by increasing the understanding of the products and processes of active volcanism. It also meets the important responsibility of contributing to the safety of island residents and visitors by keeping a constant watch on the restless, active volcanoes.

When Kilauea erupts—as it has 41 times since the Observatory has been here—the HVO staff works around the clock measuring heights of lava fountains, mapping lava flows, tracking the earthquakes and tremor that accompany eruptions, taking lava samples, analyzing volcanic gases, and assessing any hazards to life and property.

Hawaii has proved to be an almost ideal place to make these volcanic observations. Besides the fact that eruptions here are relatively frequent, Hawaii's volcanoes are accessible by road, trail and helicopter, and the felicitous climate year-round makes volcano-watching here much easier than in some parts of the world. Also, since Hawaiian lavas are extremely fluid, explosive eruptions are very uncommon. This allows the staff to work safely very near to the molten lava, taking samples and temperatures, and analyzing gases.

Between eruptions HVO closely monitors the volcanoes, with Kilauea and Mauna Loa receiving the most study. While exact prediction of volcanic eruptions is not yet possible, HVO is constantly expanding its instrument networks and improving its capabilities to detect the earliest signs of possible eruption. Data gathered from continuously recording instruments and field studies have made it possible to estimate the approximate time and general area of an eruption within hours of its outbreak; thus the National Park Service can be alerted and visitors cleared from the potential eruption areas.

Three principal techniques are most useful in forecasting eruptions: studying the record of past volcanic activity, measuring deformation, and monitoring earthquakes. The secrets of a volcano's past habits can be pieced together by studying records of past eruptions and by geologic mapping and dating the deposits from prehistoric eruptions. Future eruptions may not behave exactly as those in the past, but history is one of the better keys to the future.

Measuring deformation involves precise monitoring of changes in the volcano's surface dimensions before, during and after an eruption. As Kilauea slowly swells with magma, sensitive tiltmeters can detect the slight uplift. The Observatory uses instruments that measure changes in vertical and horizontal distances as small as one part per million.

Earthquake studies also provide vital information for determining the eruptive state of the volcano. A network of 40 seismic stations records many hundreds of earthquakes each day, mostly too small to be felt. Tens of thousands of quakes per year are detected, only about a hundred of which are strong enough to be felt by people and about 5,000 of which are large enough to be studied in detail and located accurately. A particular type of seismic tremor, known as harmonic tremor, seems to be an indication that magma is moving underground and an eruption may be imminent. When this type of tremor is recorded for a continuing length of time, an alarm is triggered in the homes of several HVO personnel if this occurs during the hours when the Observatory is not manned.

The Jaggar Museum, adjacent to the Observatory and open to the public, has dramatic exhibits on the origin of the Hawaiian Islands and their volcanic activity. Operating seismographs and tiltmeters show the ongoing earthquakes and deformation at Kilauea, and allow visitors to make their own interpretation of the current and future state of the volcano.

VOLCANOES AROUND THE UNIVERSE

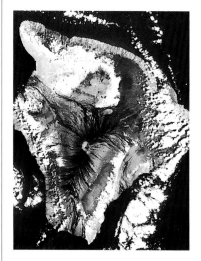

Every volcanologist has his favorite volcano. It is sometimes said that since there are fewer volcanologists than there are volcanoes, each one can have his own volcano to study, but it doesn't quite work out that way; some volcanoes are much more watchable than others.

But a volcanologist can't just study one system; he needs to study related systems, and learn from the differences between them. A major eruption finds volcanologists from all over the world hurrying to the site to make tests of their own and to exchange information and ideas with their colleagues.

Even between eruptions scientists from countries with active volcanoes cooperate on research projects and work with volcano observatories around the world. For example, there is a program at the University of Hawaii called the Center for the Study of Active Volcanoes, or CSAV (pronounced see-save). Scientists from the Hawaiian Volcano Observatory and the University of Hawaii offer instruction in volcano monitoring techniques and volcano hazards assessment to foreign participants from countries with high volcanic risk. Volcanologists from Indonesia, Philippines, Marianas, Mexico, Zaire, Papua New Guinea, Cape Verde Islands, Italy, and other volcanic lands around the world have participated since 1987.

One of the most exciting pieces of news for volcano watchers is the discovery of volcanic activity—dead and alive—on many of the planets and moons in our solar system: huge basaltic volcanoes on Mars; giant lava plains on the Moon; many volcanic landforms on Venus; and active sulfur volcanoes on Io—a moon of Jupiter. Cosmic volcano watching may be the wave of the future!

Active sulfur volcanoes dot the surface of Io, one of the moons of Jupiter.

PARICUTIN: MEXICO'S YOUNGEST MOUNTAIN

One of the hardest concepts of geology to grasp is that of geologic time; the enormous span of millions of years over which the long processes of plate movements and mountain building take place. Nature has a way, though, of revealing some of her rules and then showing us that she doesn't always have to live by them. Occasionally she will treat us to a stunning display of power in a very short time, as she did in Mexico in the 1940s when a volcano was born, grew to a large mountain and died—all within nine years.

In early February 1943, a Mexican farmer in Michoacan was plowing his cornfield with oxen and a wooden plow, as he had done for years. This time though, he noticed that the earth under his bare feet felt unusually warm, especially in a spot where there were tiny cracks in the ground. As he watched, a faint wisp of smoke rose from one of the cracks.

The farmer's neighbors and village priest were unimpressed, and told him that he had probably covered up some smoldering dry leaves. The next day, however, there was more smoke—too much to ignore. The smoke ominously and quietly increased until February 20, when a huge earthquake shook the whole valley and the earth in the cornfield was torn open.

By the time the first astounded spectators had arrived, billowing steam clouds and bursts of red-hot cinders were pouring from the cracks in the earth. At night it was a dazzling sight, with incandescent material hurled as high as 1,800 feet in the air. These rocks fell back to earth and began

to pile up around the opening, building a steep sided cone. This was the birth of a new volcano; it was named El Parícutin, the name of the nearest village.

One of the first volcano watchers to arrive on the scene was Mexico's famous painter, Dr. Atl. He was so entranced by the magnificent spectacle that he sought out the dazed farmer and bought his whole farm, including the new volcano.

Parícutin grew amazingly fast. After one week it was 550 feet high; after 10 weeks, 1,100 feet. At this stage the volcano was a true cinder cone, with no liquid lava flows.

The eruption continued in this manner for weeks, with the pile growing both in height and width. Explosive bursts were almost continuous—30 or 40 a minute—with steam and dust clouds rising to 4,500 feet and rock fragments thrown as high as 1,500 to 3,000 feet. The devastation of the surrounding area was great, not only from the encroaching pile of the volcano but from the fall of hot ashes that scorched crops and houses for miles downwind.

Then in June a new phase of the eruption began. After a long night of even more violent explosions and earthquakes, a crack opened at one edge of the crater in the top of the cinder cone, and liquid lava poured out. This was the first lava flow from the crater; it poured down the side of the new mountain, and during the next months spread out over the now-abandoned countryside.

In the next year a new cone opened on Parícutin's side and became violently active, with liquid lava flows and explosions of ash and bombs. The main crater became less active now, erupting mostly steam and gas.

As that secondary cone died, another opened on the other side of the mountain with the most spectacular lava flows of the eruption. A huge flow poured around the base of the cone and inundated a village on the other side that had so far been untouched.

The eruption continued but with gradually lessening fury, for the next nine years. The cone grew to most of its full height of 1,350 feet in the first year. After that the instability of the piled-up loose material caused slides and slumping so the volcano grew more in volume than in height. Then it died completely; Parícutin is now a silent black cone on the plain of Mexico.

Will Parícutin erupt again? Probably not. The history of the cinder cones in that area of Mexico has been for each to erupt in a single, continuing eruption and then die, with activity resuming later in a completely new spot. The farmers of Michoacan watch their cornfields uneasily for the next wisp of smoke.

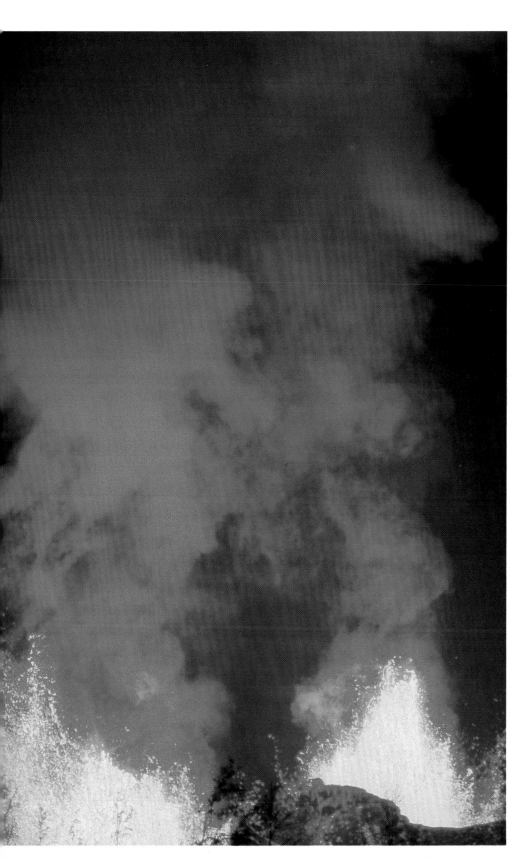

MEXICO'S VOLCANO ARTIST

olcano watching is an absorbing astime; the first Earth tremors nd whiffs of sulfur from a new ruption lure many people out to atch and wonder at Nature's ower. For some scientists it is a rofession to watch, study and each about volcanoes. But for ne Mexican painter in the first alf of this century, volcanoes bsorbed his whole life. This was Gerardo Murillo, who was always nown by the name of Dr. Atl, the ztec word for water. For him the ainting of volcanoes, the study f the science of volcanology, and is personal philosophy of life vere inextricably combined.

Mexico—like Hawaii—is a narvelous place for anyone with a bassion for volcanoes. Dr. Atl grew up in the shadow of the great volcanoes Popocatépetl nd Iztaccíhuatl. He had lived vith the volcanic shakings and umblings of the Earth, and was lways aware—both intellectually and instinctively—of how olcanoes had shaped the land and the history of Mexico.

n the early 1900s many young Mexican painters, including Dr. Atl and Diego Rivera, went abroad to study. When the Mexican Revolution broke out in 1911 they urried home and stirred the evolutionary fervor with their own contribution—the overthrow of the raditional forms of art. Dr. Atl, vith his protegees Rivera, Orozco and others, pointed Mexican art oward its folklore and fiery expressionism, and tried to encourage the artistic youth of Mexico to an awareness of the beauty of their own country. The great mural art of Mexico today vas their Revolution.

Politics could never hold Dr. Atl for long, though. (He took delight in outraging his followers by embracing—at different stages of his life—socialism, fascism, and what he liked to call anarcho-syndicalism.) He had renewed his love of volcanoes and volcanology while he was in Europe, even living for several months on the slopes of Mt. Etna. The logical place for him to go next was to the crater of Popocatépetl, the beautiful 17,887 foot smoking volcano on the edge of Mexico City. There he lived off and on for months at a time; for a period of six months he lived in a hut inside the smoking, sulfurous crater.

For Dr. Atl, the birth of Parícutin volcano in 1943 was an artist's and scientist's dream come true. He hurried at once to Michoacan where the new volcano was in fiery eruption in a cornfield, and bought it for $78. For the next nine years he devoted all his energies and talents to documenting the life of his volcano, living in a tiny hut as close as he could get to the cinder cone; ignoring explosions and the rain of hot ashes around him while he sketched and took voluminous notes.

His fascination with Parícutin was so complete that he was oblivious to his own physical condition, which was suffering greatly from the extremes of heat and cold, poisonous fumes and malnutrition. When worried friends came to look for him, they found not only that he had pneumonia, but that a neglected case of phlebitis in one leg was turning to gangrene. They hurried him off to a Mexico City hospital, where his leg was amputated. He was in grave condition for days and was not expected to live; but when one of his sorrowing friends came to see him and was refused

admittance by doctors he could hear Dr. Atl shouting "Let him in, let him in. He may die before he has another chance to visit me." Dr. Atl not only recovered, but several years later climbed to the top of Popocatépetl with one leg and a cane.

The study of Parícutin was Dr. Atl's real contribution both to Mexican art and to volcanology. Besides careful sketches and large paintings of enormous power, he kept a careful diary describing the year-by-year, day-by-day, sometimes hour-by-hour development of Parícutin.

When the eruption was finally over in 1952, Dr. Atl compiled a beautiful book which he called "Como Nace y Crece Un Volcan" (How a Volcano is Born and Grows), which included many of his drawings and paintings, scientific observations, and parts of his diary describing his experiences with a John Muir-like fervor. Characteristically, he gave the book to the Mexican government as his gift to the nation.

"Landscape," he once said, "is the tumult of the skies and the earth in a rhythm of beauty to awaken the conscience of man." In his amazingly productive career, he produced more than 11,000 drawings and 1,000 paintings, including his most famous paintings "Moving Lava," "Night View of a Volcano" and "Parícutin on Its Fourth Birthday," which are on display at the National Art Museum in Mexico City.

When Dr. Atl died in 1964 at the age of 89, Time Magazine called him "Mexico's Volcanic Volcanist" —a title that would have pleased this remarkable man.

THE TRAGEDY AT RUIZ VOLCANO

The power of a volcanic eruption is always awesome and sometimes catastrophic. The worst volcanic disaster of this century was the eruption of Mont Pelee in the West Indies in 1902, where 28,000 people were killed; the second-worst occurred at Nevado del Ruiz Volcano in Colombia in 1985.

Ruiz is a towering, ice-capped volcano in the Andes Range of South America, and the town of Armero lay at its eastern base. It was nearing midnight on November 13 and most of the 25,000 people who lived in Armero were in bed, but some were too frightened to sleep. Ominous rumblings from Ruiz had been heard earlier in the evening, and a light ashfall had dusted the streets. Geologists who had visited the town a few days before had warned of mudflows, but

most people didn't know what a mudflow was.

Suddenly, it was too late to learn. The ground shook, and with a deafening roar, wave after wave of mud, rocks and broken trees swept down the Lagunillas River into Armero. This roiling mass, with the consistency of wet concrete, engulfed and drowned 22,000 men, women and children. Sulfur fumes and screams filled the air and made it seem like hell on earth. In moments the town of Armero became a giant tomb.

What bred this awful catastrophe?

Nevado del Ruiz is 5,389 meters (17,680 feet) high, and forms the crest of a high range that rises between two major north-south valleys. Even though the volcano lies only 5 degrees north of the equator, its broad summit is covered by a large snow and ice field. Ruiz has a history of making

trouble; the Indian name for the volcano was Cumanday—the smoking nose. It had erupted violently in 1595, and in 1845 an eruption or large earthquake sent mudflows down the Lagunillas River killing about 1,000 people. Although no eruptions had been recorded since then, steam vents and a crater in the ice sheet with a small acid lake were signs that Ruiz was still alive.

A swarm of small earthquakes beneath the volcano began in late 1984. Steam emissions increased and a small explosion occurred in September 1985. A ski lodge near the edge of the ice field was closed, and warnings of the possibility of larger eruptions were sent by scientists to government officials in the towns surrounding Ruiz. However, the volcano had not erupted violently in anyone's living memory, and the few

Mudflow at Armero, Colombia.

olcanologists studying the new activity were by no means sure of their forecast. It's human instinct not to cut and run until a danger is obvious and overwhelming.

The eruption on November 13 began about 3 PM with minor explosions from the crater. Just after 9 PM the explosions became more violent, and new magma jetted from the crater in a column of hot pumice fragments and volcanic ash. Much of this hot debris landed on the snow and ice cap, causing huge floods of melt water that poured off the summit. The worst floods rushed down the tributaries of the Lagunillas River picking up soil, rocks and trees as they swept along. In places the valley sides were scoured to heights 250 feet above normal stream levels.

The steep, winding canyon of the Lagunillas River falls 13,000 feet in 35 miles before reaching the flatter country of the Magdelena Valley at the eastern base of Ruiz Volcano. Unfortunately, the town of Armero was located where the river disgorged from its steep canyon.

The mudflow torrent swept down the Lagunillas River at speeds of 35 miles per hour. At the canyon mouth where the mudflows spilled out on Armero, the waves of muddy water were nearly 100 feet high, but they quickly spread out to floods 10 to 15 feet deep. Two or three major crests of muddy water and debris flowed through Armero in 20 to 30 minutes. The deposit of dried mud left behind is about 3 to 5 feet thick and covers an area of 3 square miles. Boulders as much as 30 feet in length lie

scattered where Armero once stood.

An estimated 90% of the population of Armero were killed. Among those who survived were the people who had heeded the warnings and left town, others who lived on higher ground above the river, and a few who were swept to the thinner edges of the mudflows.

Is the current eruptive activity at Ruiz over? Earthquakes and tremor continue, and since most of the ice field was not melted by the November 1985 eruption, the danger of more mudflows still exists. A few small explosions and ashfalls have occurred

during 1986, and mudflow warning devices have been installed in the canyons high on the flanks of Ruiz. New warnings will not go unheeded.

The problem now is to give some indication of what may happen without creating panic. A new volcano observatory has been established in Colombia to monitor Ruiz. With careful watching by the volcanologists, and better understanding of the hazards by the public at risk, it is hoped that the dangers from future eruptions can be reduced.

PINATUBO, THE PHILIPPINES, 1991

When Pinatubo Volcano rumbled back to life in April 1991, no one was more surprised than the General in charge of Clark Air Base, the major U.S. Air Force installation in the Philippines. The giant runways on his base were built on flat, prehistoric volcanic deposits on the east side of Pinatubo, but everyone except a few geologists considered the volcano to be long dead. In fact, most people living in the region did not even know that Pinatubo was an old volcano. Its 1700 meter summit was eroded into a ragged ridge, and jungle covered most of its steeper slopes. It did not have the classic shape of a volcano, and was not listed in the Catalog of World Volcanoes published by the International Association of Volcanology in 1953.

All that soon changed. Beginning in March 1991, swarms of small earthquakes were felt by local residents, and the first steam explosions near the summit began two weeks later. As Pinatubo Volcano slowly awakened, no one expected that 10 weeks later, on June 15, its climactic eruption would be the second largest in this century, only surpassed by the eruption of Alaska's Katmai Volcano in 1912.

Scientists from the Philippine Institute of Volcanology, later joined by colleagues from the U.S. Geological Survey, closely monitored the increasing earthquake and eruptive activity at Pinatubo. Since more than 100,000 people lived in the region, watching the volcano was much more than a scientific exercise. Besides installing seismographs and other monitoring instruments around Pinatubo, the volcanologists also made a rapid reconnaissance of the nature and distribution of

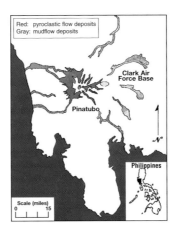

Red: pyroclastic flow deposits
Gray: mudflow deposits

Clark Air Force Base

Pinatubo

Philippines

Scale (miles)
0   15

prehistoric eruption deposits from the volcano. Both studies were disturbing; Pinatubo had a dangerous past. By radiocarbon dating of charcoal fragments in old volcanic deposits, it was determined that Pinatubo had had major explosive eruptions about 500, 3000, and 5500 years ago, and that these eruptions had poured out enormous hot ash flows, thick ashfalls, and great aprons of mudflows around the mountain—the very plains on which Clark Air Base was built.

Not only was Pinatubo's past disturbing, so was its awakening alarming. The earthquake energy kept increasing, and the location of the earthquakes migrated from a zone beneath the north side of the volcano to a more shallow, narrow zone closer to the summit. Sulfur dioxide gas emissions increased dramatically during May to more than 5000 tons per day before decreasing in early June. Small ash explosions began on June 3 and a lava dome pushed out on the northwest side of the summit on June 7, producing a steam and ash cloud 7 kilometers high. Larger explosions occurred during June 12 to 14, followed by

the gigantic eruption on June 15. Typhoon Yunya blew into the area on June 14-15, a fierce storm making bad matters worse. Since eyewitness observations were nearly impossible, much of the data about the great eruption was pieced together in hindsight. Satellite images showed that the June 15 explosions produced a mushroom cloud of ash 400 kilometers wide and 34 kilometers high. Volcanic tremor—continuous ground vibrations—and atmospheric disturbances on recording barographs indicated that the main explosive jetting of the ash eruptions lasted for about 3 hours. The volume of ash was enormous, estimated at about 4 cubic kilometers. The weight of the thick, wet ashfall caused major damage and casualties in villages and towns near the volcano; most of the 300 deaths from the giant eruption were caused by collapsing roofs.

Huge pyroclastic flows—mixtures of hot ash and gases more dense than air and flowing at high speeds—poured from Pinatubo and swept as far as 16 kilometers from the summit. These hot ash flows sterilized 400 square kilometers of land surrounding the volcano with high-temperature deposits as much as 200 meters thick. Heavy rains from the typhoon mixed with the ashfall and ash-flow deposits, and stirred up thick mudflows that poured down all the streams and rivers around the mountain.

Most residents near the volcano had evacuated before the June 15 eruption. Imagine the plight of those who had not moved far enough—daytime darkness, heavy rain and ashfall, collapsing buildings, bridges and roads washed away, lightning, thunder, the very ground and air trembling from the ongoing explosions. The miracle of Pinatubo was that it was not a worse catastrophe. To volcanologists, the forecasting of the Pinatubo eruption is a case study in things that went right.

There are 64 potentially active volcanoes in the Philippines and Raymundo Punongbayan, Director of the Philippine Institute

Explosion cloud from a large eruption of Pinatubo Volcano on June 12, 1991, 3 days before the giant climactic explosion.

of Volcanology and Seismology, takes his job with life or death seriousness. His institute established a five-level alert scheme for Mount Pinatubo on May 13, 1991, when it became evident that with its past history the ongoing unrest of the volcano posed a grave danger to the population near the mountain. Alerts increased from Level 1 (low seismicity, other unrest), no eruption imminent; through Level 4 (intense unrest including volcanic tremor and many low-frequency earthquakes), eruption possible within 24 hours; to Level 5, major eruption in progress. With good management, cooperation with local governing officials, and good luck, Punongbayan and his associates were able to convince more than 60,000 people to evacuate a zone with a radius of 30 kilometers from the summit of Pinatubo by June 14, the day before the climactic eruption. Clark Air Base evacuated 14,500 U.S. personnel on June 10, and the destruction at the installation on June 15 was so severe that no

attempt was made to renew the base contract with the Philippine Government. Although U.S. military presence in the Philippines was becoming politically unpopular, it was the eruption of Pinatubo that triggered its withdrawal.

The giant eruption on June 15, 1991 is not the end of the story. Every rainy season in the Philippines the disastrous mudflows have been repeated. The heavy rains and loose ash deposits form slurries of mud and rocks that pour down Pinatubo's steep slopes, covering with thick deposits of debris the rich apron of farmland and villages that once surrounded the mountain. In time—a few more years— these mudflows will cease, and eventually new rich soil will form on the now abandoned fields.

Volcanic eruptions on the scale of Pinatubo have definite worldwide effects. The enormous cloud of ash and gas that spewed from Pinatubo reached high into the stratosphere, above the reach of rainfall that could

wash it out. The entrapped gases that caused the explosion were rich in sulfur dioxide. Oxidized in the atmosphere to small aerosol droplets of sulfuric acid, this smudge circled the Earth in three weeks and then slowly spread over the sphere during the next year. The aerosol cloud reached its maximum worldwide distribution by late 1992, reducing the amount of sunlight radiation reaching the Earth's surface during 1992-1993. The aerosol slowly disappeared back to more normal levels by 1995. Average world temperatures dropped about 0.4 degrees centigrade during 1992-1993, bucking the trend of global warming during the past decade.

Pinatubo was an almost unknown name in 1990. Now it is notorious not only to volcanologists, but also to atmospheric scientists, to the United States military establishment, and to all the citizens of the Philippines who have suffered either directly or indirectly from its devastating economic impact.

THE CITY INSIDE A VOLCANO

The city of Rabaul lies along the curving shore of Simpson Bay, a prosperous harbor on the island of New Britain. A picturesque town of 15,000 people, its streets are lined with palms, mango and plumeria trees and its yards are bright with tropical flowers. But in this peaceful setting are some clues to the violent volcanic events that shaped this part of Papua New Guinea.

First, the rounded shape of the bay looks like a classic caldera—a volcanic basin formed by huge prehistoric eruptions and collapses. The caldera, 9 by 4 kilometers, is open to the sea on the southeast through a breach in the wall, and the resulting sheltered harbor is one of the best in the Pacific.

Other obvious clues to the island's volcanic origins are the many volcanic cones that dot the caldera's rim. Two prominent vents stand across the bay from each other, like sentinels guarding the entrance to the inner harbor. But volcanism here is hardly a surprise; Papua New Guinea lies on the Ring of Fire, the chain of volcanoes that encircles the Pacific Ocean.

Geologists think the caldera has collapsed several times in the last 10,000 years. They have found charcoal fragments in pyroclastic deposits surrounding Rabaul Caldera that give radiocarbon dates of about 500 to 600 AD for its last major collapse. That giant eruption was similar in style and magnitude to the Krakatau explosion of 1883 in Indonesia, and it was deadly to a vast area 100 kilometers in diameter. Since that great eruption, many smaller ones have built the cones scattered along the caldera rim.

In 1937 an eruption began in the shallow, near-shore waters of the caldera and built a 230-meter-high cone called Vulcan, most of it during the first twelve hours, the present known speed record for geological construction. Tragically, hot pyroclastic flows from Vulcan killed more than 500 people. Tavurvur, the other volcanic vent five kilometers across the bay from Vulcan, also erupted during the brief 1937 event. Rabaul Town escaped the deadly pyroclastic flows but was showered with seven to fifteen centimeters of volcanic ash. Plans to relocate the town were considered, but human nature, the good harbor, and the ability of tropical vegetation to make a fast recovery soon sent that idea to the file cabinets.

The Rabaul Volcano Observatory (RVO) was started in 1939 but was interrupted by the Japanese occupation of Rabaul from 1942-1945. It was opened again in 1950, and in 1973 scientists there began making some startling observations. They found that the caldera floor was bulging slowly upward; for the next decade they made careful measurements and found more than one meter of uplift. In 1983-1984 more than 90,000 small to moderate earthquakes beneath the caldera accompanied another half-meter of uplift. Since the violent history of the caldera was recognized, this unrest prompted disaster plans and practice evacuations, and drew volcanologists from all over the world. Then the earthquake count dropped from ten thousand back to tens or hundreds per month, and the uplift ceased. Fortunately all was not forgotten; RVO kept up their monitoring, practice evacuations and disaster contingency plans.

Uplift began again in 1992 but was not accompanied by a dramatic increase in earthquakes. On September 18, 1994 two strongly-felt quakes occurred nearly simultaneously beneath the caldera, producing a small tsunami in the harbor. Major uplift occurred during the night of September 18-19 but was not detected until morning; by that time Tavurvur Volcano was already erupting. With only 27 hours of seismic warning, the long-expected eruption had begun. Just over an hour after the start of the Tavurvur eruption Vulcan joined in from across the bay.

The combined eruptions dumped volcanic ash on Rabaul Town, in layers from 10 centimeters to more than 1 meter thick. Pyroclastic flows from Vulcan swept into the bay, generating tsunamis that reached as far as 200 meters onshore around parts of the harbor. Vulcan's eruption was over in two weeks, but at Tavurvur small, intermittent eruptions continued for many months.

Based on the earthquakes, a Stage 2 Alert (hazard situation possible) had been declared at 7:20 PM on September 18, eleven hours before the eruption began. A Stage 3 Alert (hazard situation probable) was declared only minutes before the eruption began. Stage 4 (evacuation required) was never announced, largely because most residents of Rabaul had begun to evacuate voluntarily during the night and early morning before the eruption started. Prompted by numerous sharp earthquakes, the majority of residents had fled to safer areas outside the caldera before 5:30 AM. By 9:00 AM, three hours after the eruption had begun, Rabaul Town was empty.

In the city destruction from ashfall was extensive; its south and east sides were listed as 100% damaged. Where ashfall was more than 0.5 meter thick almost all buildings collapsed; where it was less than 20 centimeters thick, most roofs survived. Heavy rainfall on the loose ash caused

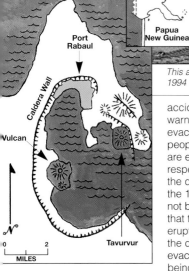

This ash-covered helicopter was stranded at the airport in Rabaul during the 1994 eruption. Tavurvur Volcano may be seen in the background.

mudflows and the tsunamis severely damaged the wharf area. Pyroclastic flows devastated the area around Vulcan but did not reach Rabaul. Luckily, the 750 people who lived near Vulcan had evacuated early.

Property damage from the 1994 Rabaul eruption totaled more than $200,000,000 but only eight people died, three of them in car accidents. With only a short warning time and no mandatory evacuation, why were so few people killed? Two main reasons are evident: First, many older and respected people remembered the deadly 1937 eruption; also, the 1984 earthquake crisis had not been forgotten, even though that time it stopped without an eruption. People remembered the disaster plans and practice evacuations, and fled without being ordered to do so.

Much has been learned about the hazards from volcanoes, but forecasting eruptions is still more art than science. Safety from volcanic hazards can never be assured. The price of living on fertile volcanic soils or near harbors that are nestled in calderas is some danger.

Was this type of earthquake swarm, uplift and eruption a bizarre incident peculiar to the South Pacific? The answer is no; the same sort of earthquakes and upward-bulging of a caldera has been measured in other parts of the world in the past fifteen years—in the Bay of Naples in Italy, with three meters of uplift, and in Long Valley, California with about one meter. That is not to say that either volcano will follow the same sequence that was seen at Rabaul; every volcano has its own story. Rabaul's best lesson is simple: It pays to be prepared.

The authors have not visited Rabaul. The above account is largely a summary of an excellent report by Russell Blong and Chris McKee (see page 84).

ATLANTIS REVISITED

Geologists and archaeologists from all parts of the world have been working together to solve one of history's oldest puzzles—the identity of Plato's lost island of Atlantis. If what they suspect is true, the Atlantis legend may have its origin in the mystically beautiful Aegean island of Thera and the huge volcanic catastrophe that happened there 3,600 years ago.

Plato described Atlantis as a large, circular island with concentric rings of land and water surrounding a rich city, all disappearing into the sea after a day and night of violent earthquakes and tidal waves. While Plato's details of the destruction don't quite fit the geology and history of the known world, some intriguing evidence is being put together that points to Thera—sometimes called Santorini—as a likely site.

The two most convincing clues are the gigantic eruption and caldera collapse of the island of Thera in 1600 BC, and the rich city buried by the eruption that is now emerging from an archaeological dig as if from a time capsule.

The eruption was massive: more than 35 cubic kilometers of volcanic debris were spewed forth in what was estimated to be about 18 hours. It began with airfall pumice lumps from a high explosion cloud, and then changed to thick glowing avalanches of pumice that were mobilized by dense clouds of hot volcanic gases. As the magma chamber emptied itself of molten rock, the center of the island collapsed into the void beneath. Where a 1,000 meter high volcano once stood, there is now an ocean-filled caldera 300 meters deep. The caldera is 10 km long and 7 km wide, more than twice the diameter of Kilauea Caldera. Today Thera is a semi-circular island forming a rocky rim surrounding the vast caldera, with a new volcanic island growing in the center.

The other clue to Atlantis is the buried city of Akrotiri on Thera's remnant shore. The archaeological diggings have so far excavated a central portion of a port city, with no edge of the town yet evident in any direction. The work moves slowly to remove the five to ten meters of pumice fall and avalanche deposits which cover the network of homes and streets. Some houses are three stories high; most contain beautiful storage jars, and all the houses excavated so far have colorful frescoes painted on the walls.

An estimated 2,000 inhabitants of the town of Akrotiri and an unknown total number who lived on the rest of the island had abandoned their homes before the giant volcanic outburst. Large ceramic jugs full of beans, grain and even sesame seeds were carefully stored away. Copper pots and household items were left behind, but all the gold and most of the weapons and tools were taken along. To where? No one knows.

Studying the layers in the excavation reveals that Akrotiri was buried by a 3-meter thick pumice fall in just a few hours. That was immediately followed by hurricane winds from volcanic blasts that covered the site with another five meters of pumice layers and great ejected blocks of solid lava the size of desks, which were ripped from the sides of the erupting vents.

No one could have survived this volcanic burial, but no human remains have been found in the streets and houses thus far excavated. The archaeologists at the dig have the distinct impression that the evacuation was well organized and carried out in an orderly fashion. People and easily-carried treasures are gone, but much of value was left behind for an anticipated return that did not occur for 3,600 years. When one walks through this silent, waiting town it is awesome to realize that it has been sealed from 1600 BC until its excavation began in 1967.

There is evidence that an earthquake caused some damage before the town was evacuated—some walls were shored up with temporary posts,

nd piles of rubble had been heaped in the streets before the eruption. But would an earthquake lead to an organized evacuation? If they survived the quake, there would be no need to evacuate; if not, there would be skeletons found and signs of panic and hasty flight.

Perhaps the volcano gave some warning shots. There is a fine layer of ash a few millimeters thick beneath the main pumice fall—a hint that the eruption may have started with minor explosions a few days or weeks before the main blast. Maybe it was the combination of an increasing earthquake swarm and small explosive eruptions that led to the evacuation. Whatever the cause, it must have been severe enough to drive people from their homes, but not so urgent as to prevent a thoughtful and organized evacuation.

No one knows whether those who fled that port city reached ships to escape, or whether the ships could have reached open sea before Thera's shores were inundated by the huge tsunamis that must have been generated by the caldera collapse. If they did survive, where did they go?

They had ships, precious goods, valuable crafts and good organization. Perhaps they cast their lot with mainland Greece to help set the stage for man's golden age?

The Atlantis legend is as mysterious and tantalizing as ever, but now there is a new trail to follow. If the fabled island has indeed been found, its impact on the beginnings of civilization, and thus upon us, will be slowly revealed in the meticulous excavations that will continue for decades to come.

MAUNA LOA'S MARTIAN RELATIVES

Mauna Loa is probably the world's best example of a shield volcano, famous for its tremendous size, gentle profile, and mild, fluid eruptions. Measured from the ocean floor, it is the world's largest mountain, taller than Mt. Everest and dwarfing it in mass. But Mauna Loa is not the largest mountain ever seen by human eyes.

Mars is the next planet traveling around the sun beyond the orbit of the Earth. It is a small, cold world only about one-half the diameter of our own planet. It is also the world of volcanic giants.

Before 1960, little was known about the geography and geology of the Red Planet. Then, three Mariner missions in 1965-1971 and the Viking expeditions in 1976 suddenly brought the solar system to our doorstep. A startling discovery is that Mars has huge shield volcanoes similar in many ways to those in Hawaii, but much larger. The largest Martian shield volcano, Olympus Mons, is 25 km (over 80,000 feet) tall, and measures 700 km (440 miles) across the base. The islands of Maui and Molokai could easily fit into the summit caldera of Olympus Mons with room to spare.

Most of the big Martian volcanoes are grouped in two regions on the northern hemisphere of the planet. The Tharsis region consists of about a dozen volcanoes and at least four major shield volcanoes, including Olympus Mons. A fifth huge volcano, Alba Patera, completes the group. Alba Patera is not a typical shield volcano, but belongs to a class that is uniquely Martian. Alba is a flat volcano with little or no relief. It is enclosed by a ring of faults and escarpments.

Near its geographic center is a large caldera with a maximum diameter of about 200 km (compared to four km for Kilauea). The average diameter of the volcano is about 800 km (500 miles). The flat profile and enclosing ring faults that truncate some of the fresh-looking lava flows suggest that while Alba was growing, it was also simultaneously collapsing. Similar paterae (saucer-type volcanoes) are scattered across the surface of Mars.

Lava flows from Martian volcanoes closely resemble Hawaiian flows, complete with lava tubes, leveed channels, and what are probably aa and pahoehoe surface textures. Some scientists believe that Martian lava may be basaltic in composition, like the lava of Kilauea and Mauna Loa. But again, everything is set to a giant's scale. Flows up to 800 km (500 miles) long and 60 km (40 miles) wide have issued from Arsia Mons, one of the Tharsis shield volcanoes. In contrast, the longest historic Hawaiian flow reaches only about 55 km.

Why do the Martian volcanoes grow so large? Most scientists believe that the Martian crust has always been too thick and rigid to break into drifting plates. Although enough heat may have been generated by radioactive breakdown in the planet's core to cause strong convection currents in the mantle, none of these currents was strong enough to disrupt the crust into drifting plates, as on the Earth. The heat that does find its way to the surface from the interior of Mars does so through hot spots analogous to the one underlying Hawaii. As the Pacific plate has drifted over the Hawaiian hot spot, a chain of over 80 shield volcanoes has resulted. But on Mars, with no crustal drift, those 80 shields add up to make one Olympus Mars, a single "megavolcano."

Imagine what Hawaii might have been like if the Earth's crust were stronger, and if the Pacific plate had remained stationary instead of drifting. A huge island could have grown, perhaps 400 miles in diameter. Mauna Loa, its single volcano, might have risen 60,000 feet above sea level. Undoubtedly, there would have been skiing all year round!

Much intrigue remains regarding the Martian volcanoes. Are basalt-like eruptive products the only volcanic rocks to be found? How old are the volcanoes, and are any still active? How have gas and steam from the volcanoes affected the Martian atmosphere? Such questions make up the mystery of volcano watching, even on worlds beyond our own.

The major island of Hawaii is dwarfed by the mass of Olympus Mons Volcano, drawn to the same scale.

100 km.

VOLCANOES AROUND THE UNIVERSE

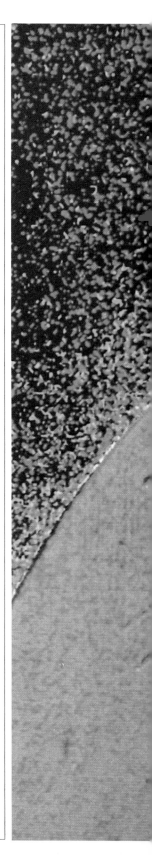

We are children of our time, our common senses tuned to our natural surroundings. This puts some severe limits on our cosmic understanding. The cold vacuum of space and the heat and super-pressures of stars are beyond our ken. We can conceive of these conditions, but we have no sense of them. For example, the chemical compound H_2O is familiar to us as ice, water, or steam, because in the common temperature and pressure ranges encountered on the Earth's surface, these various phases are stable. On the other hand, it is difficult to think of the compound of two hydrogen atoms (H_2) as anything but a very light gas used to fill balloons or dirigibles, and potentially explosive in our atmosphere which contains oxygen. But on Jupiter and Saturn there is evidence that hydrogen, the principal component of these planets, exists as a gas, deeper as a liquid, and finally as a solid under the immense pressures within these massive planets.

Ask a geologist what the most pervasive geologic process is on Earth, and he'll probably answer erosion, the tooth of time that grinds rocks to dust, mountains to mud. But how universal is this process? The present surface of the moon is apparently much the same as it has been for the last 3.5 billion years while there's hardly a trace left of our Earth's surface from that long-gone past, 75 percent of the total age of our solar system.

If erosion is not the common process on other planets, what is? The answer probably depends on the size and composition of the planet and its relation to its sun and neighbor planets, but volcanism is a good guess.

On the Earth there are about 500 active volcanoes, and in any one year about 20 of them are in eruption. They form narrow chains that occupy only a minor portion of the Earth's total surface. Sedimentary rocks cover more than two-thirds of the land surface of the Earth, and almost all but the youngest volcanic rocks on the bed of the sea. However, strip away that thin veneer, and Earth is a volcanic place. The oceanic crust is nearly all volcanic, apparently formed by submarine volcanoes along the spreading ocean ridges. Most of the continental rocks beneath the sedimentary layers are also igneous in origin, the eroded roots of ancient generations of volcanic island arcs.

Journey to the moon. There are only two basic kinds of moon rocks, volcanic rocks and broken rubble formed by meteor impacts on earlier igneous rocks. The large gray areas on the moon which are visible to the eye are called maria, or seas. They are huge lava flows billions of years old which filled basins blasted out by giant meteors. There is no proof that active volcanoes now exist on the moon. Most of the lavas brought back from the moon are older than the oldest rocks on Earth. Still, there have been occasional glows noticed by observers with telescopes. Heat flow measurements and minor moon quakes do indicate some internal processes are still active on the moon, but most planetologists agree the volcanic heyday on the moon is past.

What about the planets? Starting from the sun, Mercury's surface is similar to that of the moon, heavily cratered but with extensive areas of plains. No direct samples have

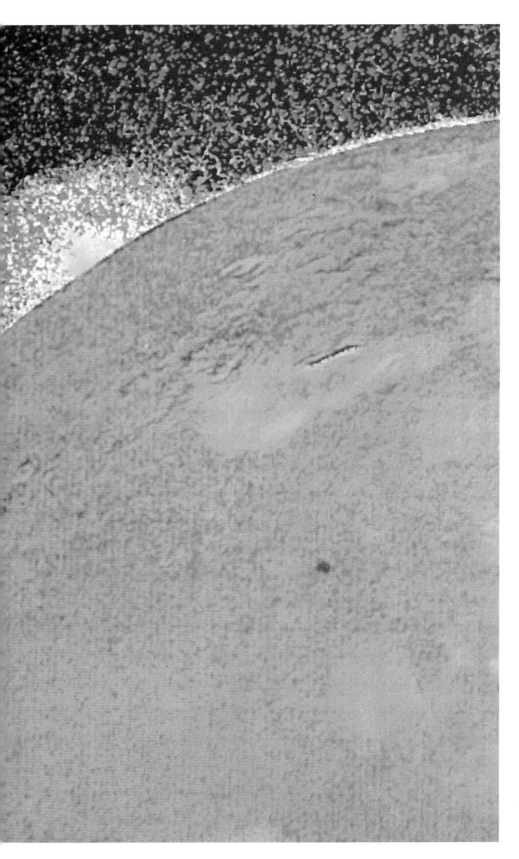

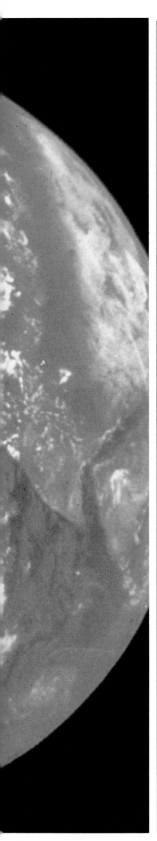

been obtained, but the smooth plains seem similar to lunar lava flows.

Venus is covered by clouds, but radar images indicate some huge craters which could be either impact or volcanic in origin. The 500°C surface temperatures of Venus are thought to be caused by sun energy trapped by high carbon dioxide concentrations in the

atmosphere. There could be active volcanoes on Venus, but the data are not yet in.

Earth we know. But when you think about how much we don't know about Earth, how much do we really know about the planets?

Mars has gigantic volcanoes, most of them apparently extinct. Olympus Mons is 25 km high, 700 km across, and its summit caldera is 80 km wide, large enough to engulf Mauna Loa. It's estimated that over 60 percent of Mars' surface is volcanic rock, ancient even by Earth's standards.

Journey beyond the asteroid belt and you come to the four great planets Jupiter, Saturn, Uranus and Neptune; all giant in diameter and light in density compared to the inner planets. The recent spacecraft fly-bys of Jupiter, called Voyager 1 and 2, discovered the most amazing

evidence yet of volcanism in our solar system. On Io, one of Jupiter's 12 moons, huge volcanoes were photographed in the act of erupting plumes as high as 320 kilometers above its mottled orange surface. Of the eight eruptive volcanoes seen by Voyager 1, six were still active when Voyager 2 passed by four months later. Temperature and composition data suggest that the volcanoes may be erupting gaseous and molten sulfur or sulfur compounds rather than the molten rocks of inner-planet volcanism. Crusting over to form solid materials, the thickening crust apparently remelts to feed the continuous volcanic cycle. Huge tidal forces from the nearby mass of Jupiter may provide the frictional heating which fuels Io's volcanism.

On Pluto and beyond, on other stars and planets what surprises await us? Could we have guessed in advance that volcanoes may be a common feature rather than something special to Earth? Perhaps so. The interiors of planets can be heated by many processes— radioactivity, tidal forces, core formation, and original heat of accretion. Planetary surfaces are chilled by the cold of space and tend to crust over. As interior materials are heated to molten form they become less dense and tend to rise, spewing out of vents onto the planet's surface. Some volcanoes of the universe mellow into fertile hills on water planets; some remain as frozen giants on sterile airless, waterless worlds.

Man has taken two vastly different views of our world. It's either very special and everything rotates around it, or it's an average planet of a second-rate star in an immense universe that is ultimately unknowable. If man is the measure of all things, there's probably some truth to both.

SUGGESTED ADDITIONAL READING

Blong, Russell and Chris McKee. **The Rabaul Eruption 1994.** Sydney, Australia: Macquarie University, 1995.

Decker, Barbara and Robert Decker. **Road Guide to Hawaii Volcanoes National Park.** Mariposa, CA: Double Decker Press, 1992.

Decker, Robert W. and Barbara Decker. **Volcanoes.** New York: W.H. Freeman and Company, 1989.

Francis, Peter. **Volcanoes.** New York: Oxford University Press, 1993.

Kious, W. Jacquelyne and Robert I. Tilling. **This Dynamic Earth.** Denver, CO: U.S. Geological Survey, 1996.

Krafft, Maurice and Katia Krafft. **Volcanoes: Fire From the Earth.** New York: Henry Abrams, Inc., 1993.

Macdonald, Gordon A., Agatin Abbott, and Frank Peterson. **Volcanoes in the Sea.** Honolulu: University of Hawaii Press, 1983.

Macdonald, Gordon A. and Douglass Hubbard. **Volcanoes of the National Parks of Hawaii.** Hawaii: Hawaii Natural History Association, 1993.

Plummer, Charles C. and David McGeary. **Physical Geology.** Dubuque, IA: Wm. C. Brown, 1996.

Rhodes, J.M. and John P. Lockwood, Eds. **Mauna Loa Revealed.** Washington, DC: American Geophysical Union, 1995.

Simkin, Tom and Lee Siebert. **Volcanoes of the World.** Tucson, AZ: Geoscience Press, Inc., 1994.

Tilling, R.I., C. Heliker and T.L. Wright. **Eruptions of Hawaiian Volcanoes: Past, Present and Future.** Denver, CO: U.S. Geological Survey, 1987.

Wood, Charles A. and Jurgen Kienle. **Volcanoes of North America.** New York: Cambridge University Press, 1991.

SUGGESTE VIDEOS

BORN OF FIRE. National Geographic Society, 1983.

INSIDE HAWAIIAN VOLCANOES. Smithsonian Institution, 1989.

KILAUEA VOLCANO: ERUPTION UPDATE. Ka Io Productions, 1996.

RIVERS OF FIRE. Hawaii Na History Association, 1985.

VOLCANO! National Geogra Society, 1989.

PHOTO CREDITS